Pictorial history of
American trucks

Pictorial history of American trucks

Niels Jansen

ELMAR

Dedicated to my wife Tineke and daughter Brenda, who saw little of me during the hundreds of hours that I spent on researching information and compiling data for this book.

Third edition 1996 by Uitgeverij Elmar B.V.
Delftweg 147, 2289 BD Rijswijk, Holland
in association with
Bay View Books Ltd.
The Red House, 25-26 Bridgeland Street,
Bideford, Devon EX39 2PZ

© Copyright Uitgeverij Elmar B.V. 1994

First Published in Dutch 1993 by Uitgeverij Elmar B.V.

ISBN 1 870979 56 7
Printed in Hong Kong

CONTENTS

Early years   9

The Twenties and Thirties   19

World War II and the postwar period   45

From the Fifties to the Seventies   65

The Eighties and Nineties   111

Author's note and acknowledgements   150

Index of illustrations   151

EARLY YEARS

By the turn of the century the mighty American continent had been settled by farmers and prospectors. Pioneers and travellers had crossed the forests, prairies and deserts in wagon trains and in the legendary stage-coaches. In the East and South, ships could navigate the larger rivers and in the mid 19th century the first continental railroads were being built. An enterprising trade spirit developed as Americans began to travel more widely. As the railroads opened up the country a lot of money was earned, but by the end of the century it was obvious that the 'New America' could not build its future on the railroads and horses and carts. Suddenly the first automobiles started to appear on the streets.

It was the automobile that forced the government to take a good look at the state of the road network. It was in very bad shape – indeed around the turn of the century there were hardly any paved roads to be found outside built-up areas, and early motorists were very restricted. Especially when the weather conditions were bad all but the most intrepid travellers were forced to stay within the city limits.

It was in this period that the forerunners of the successful American transport companies we know today were founded. For a hundred dollars you could buy a horse and cart and earn a reasonable living in the short-haul transport business, which is why it took America such a long time to switch to motorized transport. In the West it took up to the end of World War I before transport by motorized trucks became commonplace. Farmers who lived far from the cities transported their goods to the market, station or river by horse and buggy.

The cold winters in the North were another reason why automobiles were not immediately accepted, but in the big cities of the East the mechanisation of the transport business didn't take as long. Here it mirrored

Especially in the country the horse and cart remained the most popular form of transport well into the Twenties.

The first White steam-cars for goods transport were sold to a laundry company in Denver, Colorado in 1901.

developments taking place at the time in Western Europe, where the car had caught on rapidly as a new means of transport and even the first 'trucks' had appeared on the road.

The 1898 Winton Company 'delivery wagon' built in Cleveland, Ohio is seen as one of the first American built petrol engined trucks to be commercially available. In fact it was a modified automobile that could transport a limited amount of light freight and was most certainly not the first motor truck in the world as was once claimed.

In Europe Daimler had launched its *Lastwagen* in 1896 and with its maximum cargo weight of five tons this looked more like a real truck. Americans have never been too shy to exaggerate a little, and through the years we regularly find advertisements in which truck builders claim to be the first in something, or to have built the largest truck in the world. In some instances they were right, but in others their claims were a bit too

extravagant. Electric goods vehicles had been built in America since 1895, the year in which George Selden had built a prototype truck with transverse petrol engine and front wheel drive. Steam road haulage engines had also been built by then. In 1898 the first commercial vehicle was introduced in Canada, an electrically driven machine built by Fischer Equipment in Chicago for a client in Toronto.

After these first 'automobiles for transport of goods' were introduced, many other firms started to build trucks. Often they were very small companies which had previously built one or two types of automobile or had built wagons in the previous century, but they usually never got beyond the stage of producing a prototype based on an existing automobile. The American truck building industry really got under way when companies like Autocar, Mack and White came into the picture. Autocar built its first truck in 1899 (though the firm was still called the Pittsburgh Motor Vehicle Company at that stage) and in 1901 was the first truck builder to use prop-shafts, double tyres on the rear axle and, a year later, extra reduction gearing in the differential casing. In the following decades Autocar was able to claim a great number of 'firsts' in the development of the modern truck. In 1902 the Rapid Motor Vehicle Co. built a cab-over-engine truck with a freight capacity of one ton. With another firm called Reliance it formed the cornerstone of the General Motors Truck Company after GMC began its empire building in 1908.

Around the turn of the century the Mack brothers in New York started producing motorized vehicles.

In 1902 the first Mack to drive around

The Walter was based on the French Latil and had tremendous traction by 1914 standards thanks to its four-wheel drive.

wasn't a truck, but a bus that seated 18 to 20 passengers. It was initially fitted with a 4-cylinder 24HP engine, but later models received a more powerful 36HP motor that made a top speed of 20mph possible. In 1905 the firm started building truck chassis in its new factory in Allentown, Pennsylvania.

Another famous maker, White, also dates from this era: as early as 1900 the White 'delivery wagon' was developed in Cleveland, Ohio, and a year later two of these fragile trucks, with simple 2-cylinder steam engines fitted under the floor, were sold to a laundry firm in Colorado, where they caused a lot of commotion. Many a horse panicked when it met the strange-looking, hissing Whites on the streets of Denver!

White only used steam engines in the first

In 1913 this Mack truck worked side by side with horse and cart during the construction of the New York subway.

Fageol started producing trucks in California in 1916. They were fitted with 4-cylinder Waukesha engines.

White was one of the first American makes to come to Europe. In 1920 this truck was delivered to Bols in Amsterdam.

A 1913 Mack with cab over engine. After building bus chassis Mack specialized in trucks from 1905.

years of its existence, and the firm's first automobile with a petrol engine was launched as late as 1910. A year later White introduced a new series of truck chassis, from 1.5 to 5 tons, powered by a 4-cylinder 5.3 litre gasoline engine.

In 1900 Henry Ford built his first van and this could be bought for one thousand dollars. A one-tonner was introduced in 1908 based on the Model T.

Other companies that can be seen as pioneers of the American automobile industry were Diamond T (1905), Federal (1910), International Harvester (1907), Reo (1904) and Studebaker (1902). Some had been in business for a long time, but in a different sector. Most of them and their rivals were buggy or body builders and, in the case of International (McCormick), producers of agricultural vehicles. Not all the firms started out building trucks. The owner of Diamond T, Mr C.A. Tilt, built his first truck in 1911 after being asked to do so by a fleet owner who used his auto-mobiles. Soon the 1.5-ton Diamond T trucks, with 4-cylinder gasoline engines, became a

regular sight in the streets of Chicago.

Before the outbreak of World War I trucks and buses were mostly used in the big cities, motorized transport in the rest of the country being virtually non-existent because the roads were not suitable. The deep tracks made by horsedrawn wagons, as well as the steep climbs, didn't make it easy for the pioneering motorist trying to travel from one city to the other in this gigantic country.

When the seasons changed things got even worse. Heavy trucks may have taken the place of some of the horses and carts in the cities early in the century, but off the hard road they were no match at all. In rough country four horses could still pull a 10-ton load through the mud, while a 2-ton truck on cushion tyres (solid rubber but initially just steel bands) got bogged down. A lot of changes had to be made before the truck became generally accepted.

In 1903 a New York study of commercial vehicles showed that motorized transport had a future, at least within city limits. Over a period of two days the capabilities of horsedrawn carts were compared with those of trucks. The conclusion was that the latter were faster in traffic (especially on hills), had more stamina and were more economic in use than a horse and cart. The magazine *Commercial Car Journal* published a comparison of costs in 1911. It showed that a 5-ton motor truck was almost twice as expensive per day as three horses drawing a equal load, but the ton-mile cost was only half. With road improvements and the development of trucks, the difference between the two horse powers grew wider.

Body builders and trailer makers played an important role in those early years, as chassis were usually supplied bare. Well-known names from the early years are the Heil Company of Milwaukee and the Fruehauf Corporation of Detroit. The famous Trailmobile Company of Cincinnati can also be counted amongst the pioneers.

At one time every large city had a half dozen body and trailer builders, but only the best survived for more than ten years, let alone up until today.

The young Julius P. Heil founded the Heil Company in 1906 to make tanker bodies and trailers.

At first the company mainly constructed railcars, but in 1908 the first tanker to be fitted on a truck chassis left the factory, and because of good quality welding Heil tankers became extremely popular. Even the US Army

By 1918 approximately 15,000 FWD Model B cab-over-engine 3-ton 4x4 trucks had been built for the US forces.

In 1914 August C. Fruehauf designed one of the world's first widely adopted 'semi-trailers'. He reached a lot of potential customers with his slogan 'Just like a horse, a truck can pull more than it can carry'.

Truckbuilders Rapid and Reliance merged in 1911 within the infant GMC. Here we see the Pontiac, Michigan production line in 1916.

The Mack AB-Model of 1914 was influenced by Swiss Saurer designs that had been built in America, and became an immediate success. These trucks date back to 1918 and are hooked up to the first closed Fruehauf trailer design.

In 1900 Ford constructed his first commercial vehicle. A 'real' 1-ton truck based on the Model T chassis appeared in 1908, and a later example shown with ingenious dump body.

In 1904 there were only 700 trucks in America; in 1918 that number had grown to 525,000. The picture shows a White Model 45 5-ton truck of 1920.

ordered Heil tankers for White trucks used in the chase of Pancho Villa through Mexico in 1916. By the end of the decade the Heil Company was building electrically welded tankers as well as a number of other truck bodies. Mechanically and manually operated tippers joined the Heil range at a very early stage, and from 1919 onwards they were also built with a hydraulic tipping system.

Julius Heil and fellow countryman August

◄A four-wheeled trailer that could be towed from either end was a new invention from Fruehauf in 1919.

▲Goodyear started its own transport company in 1917 and bought a 5-ton Packard truck to promote its pneumatic tyres.

C. Fruehauf never became as famous as Henry Ford, but both played an important role in the development of American road transport. Shortly after the turn of the century August Fruehauf had established himself as a skilled craftsman. By 1903 operators could order a complete body for any truck on the road from his workshop in Chicago, yet Fruehauf also stayed loyal to horses as a means of transport and opened a large blacksmith shop in 1912.

A convoy of US Army White trucks in the streets of Verdun, France. During World War I over 18,000 White trucks were shipped to Europe.

Oshkosh started to build this 2-ton Model A truck in 1918. its 72HP engine and four-wheel drive made it ideal for transport over poor roads.

design and convinced Fruehauf that this design of trailer could double the freight capacity of his lumber trucks. The first Fruehauf 'semi-trailer' was born. It didn't take long for entrepeneurs to find out that a truck, just like a horse, could pull much more than it could carry. The Fruehauf Trailer Company flourished and new inventions or modifications to facilitate road transport were introduced almost every year, among them the semi-automatic coupling and the fitting of trailer landing wheels instead of the usual supports. The introduction of a four-wheeled trailer that could be pulled from both ends was another good idea from the Fruehauf engineers.

No less than 60 horses could be shoed here at the same time, which confirms that the era of the horsedrawn vehicle in America was far from over.

In 1914 a local timber merchant came to Fruehauf and asked him to build 'a thing to hitch on to my Ford Model T that will take my boat to the lake'. A few weeks later a two-wheeled trailer was ready and it was a great success. The happy owner, Frederick Sibley, immediately saw more possibilities for this

World War I accelerated the development of the truck enormously. The battlefields of Europe turned out to be the ultimate testing ground. Large concentrations of troops, thousands of tons of ammunition and other supplies were brought to the front by American army trucks. Between 1916 and 1918 the US Army bought more than 100,000 trucks from more than 200 companies. Over 18,000 White trucks were shipped to Europe, but in addition to them were 4000 Mack Model AC trucks and many other 3- and 5-ton standard 'Liberty' or 'USA' trucks. These vehicles were of simple design and not particularly comfortable to drive, but they did

In 1916 the most famous Mack of all time came onto the market: the AC Bulldog. In the picture we see a 75HP 4-cylinder chain-driven model with a couple of early Trailmobile trailers.

In the America of 1912, 461 different manufacturing companies were trying to earn a living in the truck industry. Knox was one of them and built three- and four-wheeled trucks specifically for artic operation until 1924.

their job under the most challenging circumstances. Because of their appearance and tenacious habits the AC Macks earned the nickname 'Bulldog' from the British and after the war the name 'Mack Bulldog' became synonymous with quality and longevity. In Europe everybody was impressed: the truck had proved its superiority over the horse.

If we look at American truck sales in Europe we will see that before World War I imports were virtually non-existent, and indeed many European trucks like Saurer, Commer and Thorneycroft were sold in the USA.

The big American marques had started to export their models, but Europe was not their main target, probably because the European truck industry was already well established by then. American companies published many advertisements in the foreign press, but few extra sales were realized, and it was at least another ten years before a good number of American trucks could be seen on European roads. Apart from direct imports there were also lots of army surplus trucks for local operators to use after 1918. By 1920 hundreds of Federal, GMC, Mack, Packard, White and other 'Liberty' army surplus trucks had found new owners in Europe. As a consequence road transport was stimulated enormously. Factories refurbishing FWD and Peerless chassis in Britain developed into manufacturers in their own right and similar things happened in France and elsewhere.

In the meantime the truck had also earned

Sterling taught truckers how to handle their machines by publishing a series of colourful advertisements around 1920.

In the early years most roads were unsurfaced and a trip of a few miles often took a long time.

its place in America. In 1904, the first year of registration, there were only 700 trucks in use. By 1918 this number had risen to more than 525,000. The statistics on truck producers are also interesting. After a slow start around the turn of the century there were over 100 American truckbuilders active in 1907. Only five years later, in 1912, the sector reached its all-time best with no less than 461 different makes of trucks.

Most of these so-called manufacturers stemmed from forges, body and wagon builders and even bicycle makers wanting to try their hand at constructing a delivery wagon. You could almost find them on every street corner and at one moment there were 37 cities, led by Chicago, Detroit and New York, with more than 100 truck producers each.

This phenomenon existed because the motorized transport of goods was limited to the big cities. The first trucks were never far away from home, and the closer a truck operator was to the builder, the better. The majority of small makers disappeared just as quietly as they had appeared, but *Commercial Car Journal* still listed 64 different truck advertisements in its November 1919 issue. Trucks had become big business in a very short time.

THE TWENTIES AND THIRTIES

World War I had proved in Europe and America that the modern truck was essential for transporting large numbers of people and goods quickly and economically. Heavy trucks with a load capacity of 3, 5, 7 or even 10 tons seemed to have a future, but something had to be done about the roads first. In 1907 the American government created a road construction department, but it took until 1915 before the roads really started to be improved on a national scale. Most of the financing of this project was met by local authorities, who concentrated on the improvement of roads within their city limits. Anything planned for renewal outside was less important. In one instance a number of truck builders even proposed to finance and design a main road, the Lincoln Highway. The railroads didn't help matters and were extremely powerful when it came to lobbying against the roads.

Ford has always been a bestseller on world markets. This Model BB truck is seen in South Africa.

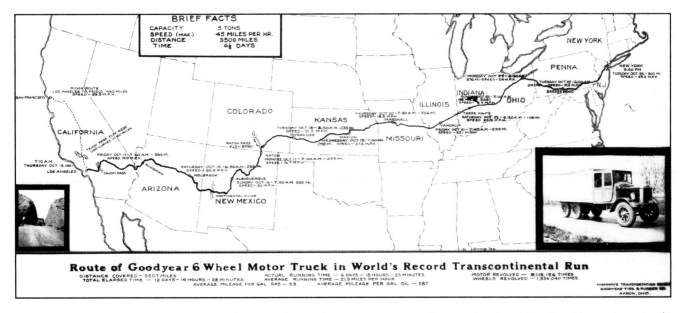

In 1921 Goodyear designed 6-wheel trucks that started a regular coast-to-coast service, crossing the 3500 mile wide continent in 6½ days.

Pierce-Arrow was best known for its exclusive motorcars, but also built heavy trucks from 1910 to 1932. It was latterly linked with Studebaker until acquisition by White in 1932. This semi-trailer outfit from about 1924.

The war required more and more transport facilities and by 1917 the railroads could not meet all the demands. That is why the government finally gave priority to building roads between the larger cities in the East. The truck now had the opportunity it needed to prove itself.

It was also promoted as a means of long-haul transport from another angle. The Goodyear Tyre & Rubber Company had been trying to sell its new pneumatic tyres to truckers for years but had not had very much success, because most trucks were driving around on old-fashioned cushion tyres. For short-haul traffic within the city these were adequate, but to prove that a truck would do better on pneumatic tyres - especially on longer trips - Goodyear founded its own

transport company in 1917: the legendary Wingfoot Express.

A 5-ton Packard truck was purchased. It was fitted with extra fuel tanks and carried spare parts, an air compressor and a set of spare tyres. The cab was fitted with a bunk behind the driver's seat, a completely new concept in those days. The first journey, with a few tons of Goodyear tyres aboard, was from Akron, Ohio to Boston, Massachusetts.

On the return trip raw materials for the tyre industry were carried. The 1500 mile route wasn't in very good shape and due to being bogged down in the mud and engine trouble the journey took 23 days. Learning from this the return journey was made in 5 days.

After tyre improvements and with drivers becoming more experienced, Wingfoot Express became a serious competitor to the railroads. Goodyear proved that pneumatic tyres were suitable for road transport and had many advantages on rough terrain. They did not break up the road surface and trucks didn't get bogged down in mud or sand as much as in the past. The trucks themselves became more reliable too, and in 1918 Wingfoot Express even started a regular service from Boston to San Francisco, a distance of 7800 miles clear across the continent. It was a gruelling challenge for both man and machine, and in the state of Wyoming 36 of the 56 bridges they had to cross caved in under the weight of the truck, yet after four journeys Wingfoot Express managed to offer a 14-day transcontinental freight service.

This is how ice was transported in 1927 using a 7-ton Packard.

In 1928 Hansa started a regular service using White Series 50 trucks from Holland via Hamburg to Berlin in Germany, a 1000-mile round trip.

Sterling F-Series trucks were strong and handsome in 1931. The yearly production typically exceeded 1000 around this time.

Le Moon is a lesser known make, but for almost 30 years a number of interesting models were built, such as this 1931 12-ton tandem-axle truck powered by a staight-eight Lycoming engine.

Thanks to these experiences the development of the truck tyre was stimulated. To carry more weight, tyres were enlarged up to the point where any further increase in size would be impractical, and the Goodyear engineers found a solution by placing two rear axles behind each other – the tandem-axle truck was born. Goodyear was still using Packard trucks, but had added Mack and White vehicles to the fleet. In 1920 its tandem-axle truck was on the road and more followed, including a bus. Wingfoot Express used these trucks up to 1926 for their coast-to-coast service, often with a four-wheeled trailer behind.

Other tyre companies like Firestone and Goodrich, as well as component suppliers,

The artistic posters that Mack and other makers printed in the Thirties gave the impression that the transport sector would benefit the economy.

An impressive Mack AC tank combination in Maryland, 1929.

body builders and truck producers themselves now saw a chance of combining to overwhelm the railroads' supremacy.

In 1920 there were 1.1 million trucks on the road; seven years later that figure had virtually tripled. By fitting pneumatic tyres and improving the roads in the industrialized East, the truck got its chance to beat the train in terms of speed. Within city limits a speed of 25mph was already much faster than the horse and cart, but to operate successfully in the lucrative long-haul market more powerful engines were needed.

The first large 6-cylinder engines first appeared in buses. In competition with the railroads the intercity bus lines kept on adding more horsepower to their 'high-speed' buses. Powerful 6-cylinder engines, with high gear ratios, were finally also used in trucks in the late Twenties, and because of the development of buses, some trucks were now able to reach a speed of 50mph or more. The greatest problem was braking distance: buses and trucks became faster and faster, but stopping was another matter! Things improved when Westinghouse introduced the first pneumatic brakes for trucks in 1921, and

A rare sight in Europe, a Republic of around 1927 vintage with its proud Dutch owner.

Sterling was one of the first to start building heavy trucks in the East and these soon became popular on the West Coast too. This is a 1929 chain-driven Model DC-25-64 in California.

in 1925 GMC went a step further by fitting this type of brake to all four wheels.

In the same period the first intermediate 3-speed Brown-Lipe gearboxes, Timken double-driven rear axles and Hendrickson tandem suspension units were also developed.

In the beginning most of the trucks had the steering wheel, or 'tiller', on the right but in the early Twenties a switch was made to left hand drive. The general appearance of the truck had also changed, and the bench over the engine that was the driver's seat disappeared. With the odd exception the driver sat behind the engine. Chain driven trucks were followed by trucks with a propshaft, although some marques like Mack and Sterling produced chain driven trucks up to the Fifties.

Electric headlights and a closed cab became standard and every new model incorporated some form of major innovation, usually in the drive line. Truck builders were looking for

better performance and for developments that would improve the versatility of their trucks for multi-purpose transport.

In 1921 serious plans were made to construct a national highway network. Dwight Eisenhower once led a military convoy across the country and saw that strategic road transport was impossible until something had been done to improve the quality of the roads. Plans were made for the construction of an Interstate Highway network with a total length of 56,000 miles. By 1925 a quarter of this plan had been realized, and even the Depression of the Thirties didn't halt the development of the road system, as President Roosevelt gave the building of roads priority to keep tens of thousands of people at work.

Every self-respecting truck builder designed a number of chassis for road construction purposes and for municipal services. Large companies such as Autocar, GMC, Federal, International, Mack and White advertised

This Mack Model BJ with integral sleepercab is a beautiful example of an early owner-operator rig. Note the many extras such as the canopy over the side window, air horns, spotlights, etc.

A well restored 1929 Fageol. Fageols were easy recognizable by the large louvres on the hood.

A beautiful 1930 Hendrickson Six-Wheeler. In the mid-Thirties Hendrickson tandem-axle suspension systems were fitted to International trucks, and from 1948 were also supplied to other makers.

Michigan-based Acme built truck and bus chassis with 4- and 6-cylinder Continental gasoline engines until 1931.

their trucks as being the best for building a trans-continental network of roads. Some of the smaller truck factories like Nash, FWD and Oshkosh had developed four-wheel drive trucks that proved themselves in the barren country outside the cities and had given useful wartime service. Government departments began to see more advantages in the heavier trucks. Fitted with snow-ploughs, the all-wheel drive FWD and Oshkosh trucks proved to be indispensable in keeping the growing stream of traffic moving on the roads of the East.

In the mountain states on the other side of the continent the roads were in worse shape. Trucks had a lot of trouble traversing the old Indian trails right up to the Thirties, and in winter the roads could not be kept free of snow. Some of the large transport companies like Consolidated Truck Lines (later Consolidated Freightways) had no other choice but to fit their own heavy Kenworth and Fageol trucks with snow-ploughs to do the job, while up to World War II drivers in the barren Northwest had to cope with a lot of mud and dust.

Many people say that the best and most reliable trucks were built on the West Coast: the great marques Fageol, Kenworth and Peterbilt wrote history here. The Californian

Fageol Motors Company started out in 1916 by making many types of vehicle but soon settled on trucks and low level Safety Coaches. They kept it up until 1938, when Sterling took over all the shares. Thus this well-known company from the East managed to get a foothold in the West. Sterlings were just as reliable and strong as Fageols and Kenworths, and became just as popular over the years. Another famous marque, Peterbilt, was founded in 1939 when T.A. Peterman bought the old Fageol factory from Sterling, so it was no coincidence that the first Peterbilt models had a lot in common with the last Fageols.

An important competitor, Kenworth, was founded in 1923, when two ex-directors of the Gersix Manufacturing Company of Seattle started their own business. In the early years Kenworth built trucks up to 5-ton capacity and fitted them with powerful engines, but with an annual production of under one hundred trucks in 1925 they were still trailing the market.

The mountainous roads and long distances in the West needed reliable and strong trucks which in addition had to pull longer and heavier trailers than elsewhere in America. When the diesel engine was introduced in the Thirties, Kenworth was the first to offer a 4-cylinder 100HP Cummins diesel engine as an ex-works option, in 1932.

A year before, Clessie Cummins, had proved, in a number of coast-to-coast test-drives, that diesel engines had many advantages for the trucking world, especially as far as fuel consumption was concerned. An Indiana truck with a Cummins diesel engine was able to travel a distance of 3200 miles using only $11.22 worth of fuel. Petrol engines

A nicely rebuilt 1931 Mack AC chain-drive six-wheeler in Canada.

Kenworth came into existence when two ex-directors of Gersix in Seattle went into business for themselves. In 1932 Kenworth was the first to offer the 100HP Cummins diesel engine as an original factory option.

A heavy 6x6 FWD fitted with a Heil sludge pump, 1930.

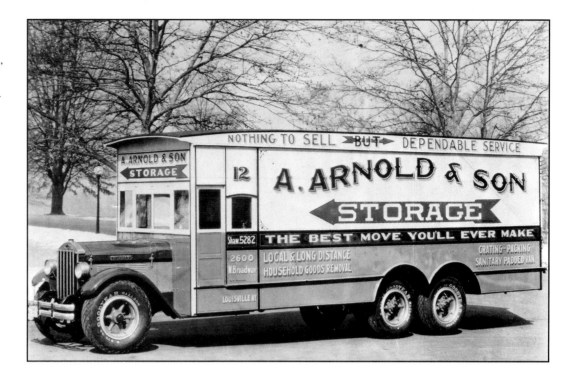

A 1929 Diamond T six-wheeler. In that year more than 3 million 'motor-trucks' were already registered in the USA.

In 1912 one of the Mack brothers, Jack Mack, started a truck factory with Roland Carr and they built trucks up to 1935. The picture shows one of their 1931 Maccar trucks, a Model 86A.

for trucks and buses have been more popular in the States than elsewhere in the world, because of low fuel costs, but in the Thirties many transport companies switched to diesel, not only for their lower fuel cost, but also for their torque on long gradients, reliability and low maintenance costs.

In the meantime the development of other truck components continued, and it is interesting to note that a number of things we see on trucks today had already been thought of in the Thirties.

Hendrickson designed a heavy three-axled COE (Cab Over Engine, or forward control as

this layout is know in Britain) with sleeping accommodation above the driver's seat as early as 1932. This was the predecessor of the topsleeper. In the Twenties Californian trucks were fitted with an extra trailing rear axle to comply with local requirements. The heavy GMC Model T-90 of 1930 could be delivered with an adjustable steering wheel as an optional extra. There were even disc-brakes: California truck builder Moreland offered discs as an optional extra on its new 1936 R-Model 'conventional' (an American term for a truck with hood-or bonnet in Britain).

Aerodynamic trucks are quite common

Large numbers of trucks were used in road construction. Here we see a rare Reiland-Bree in Illinois in 1931.

A real classic is this 1931 Mack AK six-wheeler with trailer. The big rig had a hauling capacity of 34 tons, which made it one of the heaviest trucks on Pennsylvanian roads at the time.

A 1932 International Model A-8 powered by a 6-cylinder 136HP gasoline engine. To carry more freight two trailers were hooked up behind the tractor.

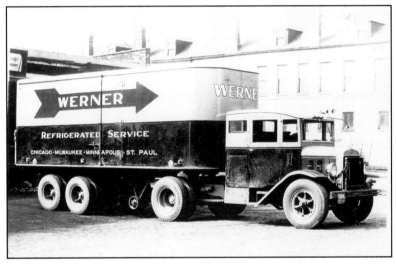

A 1932 Available sleepercab tractor pulling an Available tandem-axle trailer. This Chicago-based manufacturer built 50-100 trucks per year, the last in 1957.

today, but integrated sleepercabs, various front and side fenders, roof spoilers and streamlined trailers could be seen on American roads in the Thirties.

Body and trailer builder Heil made a beautiful stainless steel milk tanker in 1927 and in 1934 its first fuel tanker saw the light. A further all-new range of very good-looking streamlined Heil tankers was introduced just before World War II, and the company also designed the first aluminum tanker trailer, aluminium having already proved itself as a

suitable material for other types of truck bodies. Fruehauf made its first all-aluminium trailer in 1934. After the introduction of more powerful engines, trailers became heavier and heavier, and trucks often pulled more than one. These products were built by Fruehauf, Great Dane, Heil, Highway, Trailmobile and countless smaller firms which mainly operated locally.

In order to offer a complete product line companies like GMC, Kenworth and Mack for years constructed trailers as well as trucks.

In 1932 Schacht offered a range of trucks topped by the 10-ton Series TR-H, powered by 6-cylinder Hercules or Wisconsin gasoline engines with a 5-speed overdrive transmission.

In Holland, during the thirties, not even a thousand truckchassis were sold yearly. Nevertheless business went well for Englebert's Automobielhandel – a Dutch dealer – thanks to International's popularity.

This 60 year old Mack was still in use in 1992, but the original engine had been replaced by a 210HP Cummins V8 diesel.

Also on the West Coast, where GVW (Gross Vehicle Weight) started to play an ever greater role because of stricter legislation, the likes of Kenworth, Fageol and Sterling produced many truck components of aluminium instead of steel.

During the Thirties the American truck was modernized at an ever increasing pace. In the preceding decade functionality had prevailed over styling, but ten years later most truck builders could offer a model range with sleek hoods and streamlined cabs. Light and mid-sized trucks from Chevrolet, Diamond T, Dodge, Federal, Ford, GMC, Indiana, International, Stewart and Studebaker used styling that was comparable with that of contemporary automobiles.

The really heavy trucks remained faithful to old designs, typified by the square 'longnose' with a cube shaped cab. In the mid-Thirties there was a tendency to change back to the COE (Cab Over Engine) models, to gain increased loadspace where there were maximum length limitations in the East. A number of these models became popular in export markets too, like the Diamond T COE type V in 1937 and the slightly earlier White 800-Series COE.

These established American marques could also count on a number of faithful European transport companies which were impressed by the reliability of their trucks and the good service provided by local importers.

Road transport boomed in the Old World in the Twenties and the Americans played an important role in this development. Look at

Because of their reliability, longevity and soft suspension American trucks were extremely popular in Europe prior to World War II. A number of them have been lovingly restored.

An Indiana Model 85 tractor with locally made bodywork and semi-trailer. After a period under Brockway control Indiana passed to White in 1932 as a cheaper assembled alternative range of trucks.

In 1933 Chevrolet was the best selling truck. This unusual tandem-axle model LS with 6-cylinder gasoline engine could haul a good load of beer.

the Amsterdam motorshow of 1928: of the 35 truck builders that were present, more than a third were American companies. The familiar makes like Chevrolet, Dodge, Ford, GMC, International and Studebaker became popular because of their reliability, longevity and good qualities on the road, but in the course of time a lot of lesser known American marques were exported to Western Europe as well. Examples include Brockway, Condor, Federal, Indiana, Republic, Stewart and Willys. The Americans tried hard to gain a part of the lucrative commercial vehicle market, but

were hampered by import restrictions until some established local assembly operations, notably in Britain which of course spoke the same language.

Of all American trucks Ford took the largest share of the European market, and that remained the case until 1960. Ford led Chevrolet, Dodge and GMC, mostly due to price and not any difference in quality. There were plenty of transport companies that would have loved to own a Diamond T or a White, but they were simply too expensive.

It is interesting to note that some advertisements abroad for the Diamond T of the Thirties stated that the truck 'could easily carry twice the stated maximum load' – a regular expectation in countries where overloading was the norm.

Because petrol was already becoming more expensive in Europe than America, assembly companies began looking for alternative power sources. From 1933 Albatros in Holland fitted 4- and 5-cylinder British Gardner diesel engines in heavy White chassis.

A few years later a number of European truck operators purchased White 700-Series chassis fitted with the German Junkers 4-, 6- and 8-cylinder two-stroke diesel engines. The combination of a reliable and luxury American chassis with an economical European diesel engine proved a popular choice in the Thirties for transport companies with money to invest.

In less than twenty years the truck had evolved from a motorized wagon to a fast and efficient means of transport.

In 1928 Hayes in Canada started the production of heavy trucks mainly for the logging industry. Here we have a rare highway truck from the early days when they were called Hayes-Anderson.

Brockway was one of the largest independent truck builders in the USA at the beginning of the Thirties. Here we see a Model 160 while changing Fruehauf trailers.

The 691 with
6-cylinder engine and
5-speed gearbox was
the heaviest truck
White built in 1933.

A robust White Model 64 in 1933.

Beers of Holland started importing Diamond T trucks in 1931. Because of their good looks, robust construction and strong 6-cylinder Hercules engines they soon became very popular.

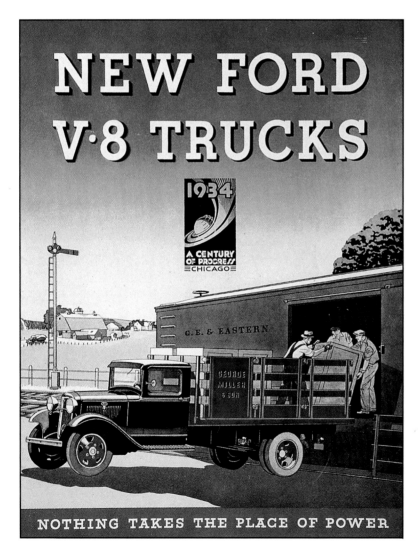

◄The new Model BB truck with 3.6-litre 65HP V8 petrol engine regained Ford's place as No. 1 truck manufacturer in 1934.

► In 1934 General Motors built this magnificent GMC T-96 Six-Wheeler with GMC trailer, powered by an 11.7-litre 6-cylinder 173HP gasoline engine.

Kenworth is best known for its heavy trucks, but in the Thirties it also designed lighter models.

A nice 1934 Mack BQ beer wagon. Only 327 of this heavy type with 128HP 6-cylinder gasoline engine were built.

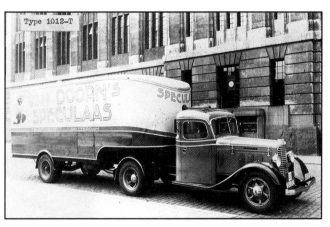

In 1934 Diamond T launched this sleek model. The combination of good looks and sturdiness made it very popular in export markets.

The roomy interior of
a mid-Thirties White
conventional.

A major Dutch warehouse chain bought this handsome locally bodied White
707 in 1934.

Through changes in
legislation the cab-
over-engine design
became more popular
in the Thirties. Here
we see a 1934 GMC T-
74-H-C pulling Heil
tank doubles with a
GCW of 50 tons.

In the second half of the Thirties the majority of trucks became more streamlined, like this fine 1935 6-cylinder Federal semi.

In 1936 the demand for diesel engines led a Dutch importer to offer 165HP German Junkers two-stroke engines in big White 700-Series chassis.

One of the more unusual makes coming to Europe was the Condor. In America similar trucks were sold under the name Gramm.

Reo Speedwagons were popular in Canada. This model with trailing axle was powered by a straight-eight gasoline engine and is shown in service in 1936.

Between 1936 and 1938 Reo built seven Junior types for Mack. You didn't see many of them operating as long-haul rigs.

The poor mountain roads of the West Coast were a tough assignment for Consolidated Freight Lines' Fageol trucks. Large 150HP Buda or Waukesha engines coupled to 12-speed Brown-Lipe transmissions gave them the necessary power and traction.

Brockway made trucks with advanced styling in 1936. This is a Model 160X sleepercab tractor pulling a Fruehauf van trailer.

The 'snub nose' CJ model was Mack's 1933 answer to the demand for cab-over-engine designs. In 1937 the cube-shaped cab was replaced by a more streamlined one.

This stylish 1937 GMC COE operating in England received a local cab and tank made by Bonallack.

▼ In Western states it was common to see giant rigs such as this impressive 1937 Autocar Diesel model NF 6x2 truck and trailer.

Concrete roads were still a rarity in the Thirties. An Interstate Highway system had yet to be devised, but the threat of war made the government speed up the idea of linking the nation together.

While roads remained poor Oshkosh did good business. The robust FB series 4x4 was kept in production until 1942. They were mostly used for road building and snowploughing.

The Mack ER was a limited edition model. This heavily laden 1937 Californian truck and trailer sports a trailing axle and chain drive.

Ford trucks were extremely popular in Europe. This V8 model of 1937 is seen pulling a locally built trailer in Holland. Chevrolets were successful too and these gave rise to the popular UK-built Bedfords of the 1930s.

In 1937 body builder Gar Wood designed this beautifully streamlined Texaco tanker on a GMC six-wheeler chassis.

From 1935 onwards Kenworth trucks could be easily recognized by their long hood with traditional grille. The contemporary W900 model still shows this heritage.

The heavy Mack BX1 was built for eight years. The picture shows a milk tanker of the Bowman Dairy. In 1938 50 million tons of milk were produced in America.

Fageol built this last heavy conventional just before their takeover by Sterling. The latter retained the service network, but sold the production rights on to T.A. Peterman.

With the blueprints of the latest Fageol model in hand T.A. Peterman built his first Peterbilt truck in 1939.

Studebaker produced a series of sleek long-nosed trucks in the late Thirties. The styling reflects that of contemporary cars.

This is a 1939 Autocar NF with a Trucktor trailing axle. The tanker was designed by Heil and had a capacity of 3150 gallons, divided into nine compartments.

Sterlings were not only reliable but they also exuded prestige and good quality. This is a chain-driven sleepercab tractor of the H-Series from 1939.

International's truck range was renewed in 1937. In the picture we see a model D-35 with a 1939 vintage Wilson van trailer.

When the war broke out there were 4,590,386 trucks registered in America. Of all manufacturers White had the largest share of the heavyweight market.

Marmon-Herrington was renowned for its all-wheel-drive Ford conversions in the Thirties and Forties. The firm also produced its own heavy 4x4 and 6x6 trucks, of which many were exported.

Before the war GMC's Oldsmobile also constructed a few trucks, usually for export only. This three-axle dump truck had a 6-cylinder 3.8-litre gasoline engine and similar styling to GMC's cars.

A Federal with a Fruehauf trailer from the mid-Thirties. As we can see on
the license plate, it was still at work in 1948.

WORLD WAR II AND THE POSTWAR PERIOD

Long before the World War II the truck industry was confronted with a changing world. The threat of war made the US government anxious to speed up construction of a network of roads because it appreciated the role trucks could play in the defence of the country. In 1939 a decision was taken to increase the amount of strategic highways from 26,000 miles to 75,000 miles in total, of which 29,000 miles should be modified or reconstructed immediately. In the existing network no less than 2400 bridges were too weak to carry heavy civilian or military trucks.

The greatest problem was that each state had its own legislation concerning the maximum size and weight of trucks, and some of these laws had not kept up with developments in the truck industry. In the Forties five states still calibrated the maximum permissible weight of a truck by measuring the width of the tyres. This had carried over from the times when trucks still used cushion tyres. In 1941 four-wheeled trucks with air-filled tyres in Texas were not allowed to weigh more than 8.5 tons, while in other states the maximum was 18 tons. In 1942 the so-called federal trainweight was imposed for the duration of the war, but when it was over the states went back to their own individual rules. This chaotic situation would last until the Eighties!

In technical terms, trucks at the end of the Thirties were capable of carrying a considerably heavier load than was permitted during the war and transport companies were thriving. To keep the defence industry going a lot of people and goods had to be transported all over the continent, and a blind eye was turned to the odd extra ton loaded. In 1937 the ICC rules, which controlled the licensing of trucks and driving times, were also temporarily suspended, and after the war the ICC (Interstate Commerce Commission) became a disputed organization.

By 1940 trucking was big business, with around 4,5 million trucks registered. An interesting detail is that one quarter of that total were being used in the agricultural sector.

For example in 1940 no less than 37 million gallons of milk were transported daily by trucks, and in the same year trucks transported 4,557,000 crates of eggs to Chicago.

Some 54,000 American towns and cities became dependent on trucks because there was no alternative means of transport.

The industry was growing all the time. Just before the war the famous marque Peterbilt

Just before the war Sterling designed the striking J series conventional. This model was built with either chain or shaft drive and operators could choose between gasoline and diesel engines.

In 1940 Chrysler Corporation built Dodge, DeSoto and Fargo trucks, which all resembled each other. More than 60,000 Dodges were sold per year.

▲ In 1938 Dutch Kromhout became a licensee of Autocar and assembled a number of medium-duty trucks in Holland. A few years later this operation was also able to offer the heavier Autocar C-50 model.

(as discussed with Fageol) came on the market, followed in 1940 by Freightliner, which was a case of an operator building trucks for its own use. Thermo King developed its first mechanical refrigerated trailer and Fuller introduced its first Roadmaster transmission in 1941, by when GM's Detroit two-stroke diesels were proving their worth.

In 1939 two large American transport companies started designing their own trucks: Consolidated Freightways in the Northwest and Horton Motor Lines in the East. When road transport started to increase on the West Coast in the late Thirties, Consolidated

In 1940 International Harvester Co. produced approximately 86,000 trucks, among them this handsome DR-700 cab-over-engine type.

Freightways founder and director Leland James decided to design a new truck that would stand up to the requirements of the West. The Kenworth and Fageol trucks that were used until then were extremely reliable, but too heavy. James and his associates designed a tandem-drive truck with a tandem-axled trailer which had an enormous load capacity while remaining relatively light and strong. They chose a COE layout and used as much aluminium as possible. Consolidated didn't plan to build these trucks themselves, but because they couldn't find a truck builder that would accommodate them, they decided to open their own truck building plant in 1940.

The spin-off Freightways Manufacturing Company in Utah was born. With the assistance of Alcoa, which already had a lot of experience in building aluminium truck bodies, nine Freightways trucks were built in that first year. In 1941 the name was changed to Freightliner, but the factory in Salt Lake

A 1940 Kenworth COE with 6-cylinder Hall-Scott gasoline engine. The model was also offered with a 225HP underfloor engine.

Impressive Sterling model HCS-255 fitted with a 12 cube Heil dump body, 1940.

The White WA series COE followed on from the 800 and was powered by a 6-cylinder gasoline engine rated at up to 130HP.

Freightliner COE trucks and trailers were also sold to other transport companies. In the Fifties they were extremely popular on the West Coast, where heavier trucks and trailers were permitted. To cross the mountains in the West these trucks were fitted with powerful 275HP Cummins supercharged diesel engines and Fuller or Spicer multi-speed gearboxes.

Consolidated Freightways had more than 20,000 trucks on the road in 1992 and is the third largest transport company in the USA, after Roadway Express and Yellow Freight. And they have always used Freightliner trucks.

City closed in 1944, having produced 38 trucks and as many trailers. Three years later five ex-employees started building trucks again in Portland, Oregon. In 1947 and 1948 the total output was purchased by Consolidated Freightways, but later

Another transport company that preferred building its own rolling stock to buying it from others was Horton Truck Lines. Until 1953 a sister company of Horton built the Brown truck, named after its chief engineer. Initially it was exclusively for use by Horton, but from 1945 onwards the basic trucks, with hood or as a COE, were also on offer to other transport companies. They were never very cheap and that is the main reason why production of these beautiful and robust trucks ceased after over 1000 had been produced.

The large Kenworth longnose was facelifted in 1940 and got an upright radiator grille. The new model was well received but with a yearly production of only 226 units Kenworth remained one of the smaller truckbuilders.

Due to World War II the large scale production of standard trucks grew enormously. Since 1946 at least one million trucks and buses have been produced yearly (except for under 900,000 in 1958). 1.5 million was exceeded for the first time in 1964 and 2 million in 1971.

During the war General Motors Corporation built 854,000 trucks and amphibians, 38,000 tanks and 198,000 diesel engines. It also built a lot of other equipment for the needs of war. Marques like Autocar,

Federal had a big success during World War II with its heavy 6x4 and 6x6 wreckers and tankers, but the production of civilian trucks like this Model 85 remained important.

Mack was still advertising the old AK Bulldog in 1937. A total of 2819 units was produced from 1927 onwards.

Streamlining was fashionable, as this 1937 Federal model shows.

When weights went up, Fruehauf designed a new line of monocoque trailers in 1938.

Diamond T trucks of cab-over-engine design were imported into Europe but never sold as well as the conventional models.

Biederman, Brockway, Chevrolet, Corbitt, Diamond T, Dodge, Federal, Ford, GMC, International, Mack, Pacific, Reo, Studebaker, Ward LaFrance, White and a few more could all be seen in olive drab. Every truck factory worked 24 hours, seven days a week, to fill the demand for military trucks.

For factories that specialized in 'all-wheel-drive' products, like FWD, Oshkosh and Marmon-Herrington, this was a time in which they could really prove themselves. Without

4x4 and 6x6 trucks the famous Alaska Highway, built through the wilderness by the army in record breaking time in 1942, would still be a dream. A lot of the successes on the battlefields themselves can also be attributed to the hundreds of thousands of trucks that were deployed.

Without that logistic support the war could never have been won. The American and Canadian truck factories produced a combined total of 2,600,887 military trucks

A Mack LHSW six-wheeler with trailer of the Bowman Dairy Company in Michigan. Their fleet of 2100 trucks made them one of the largest milk transporters of the country.

and 529,647 trailers in wartime. The technical developments in the war years were enormous and the infrastructure was substantially improved.

In Canada the Forties and Fifties were still pioneering years for road traffic, apart from the Alaska Highway. In 1946 a party of army officers succeeded in crossing Canada from east to west by road for the first time. Even today there is still only one main road connecting Ontario and Manitoba, the Trans Canada Highway. Canada is generally thinly populated and its road transport cannot be compared with that of the States. In 1945 the 12 million inhabitants of Canada were served by 300,000 trucks.

Of course American trucks have always sold well in Canada, but there have also been some interesting indigenous designs. Usually these were heavy trucks built for hard work in the mines, forestry or oilfields. The best known marque is Hayes, which started producing robust rigs and trailers for lumber transport in 1922 under the name Hayes-Anderson. In the Thirties this company had good contacts with England and often used Leyland and Rolls-Royce engines. After a spell of Mack involvement the firm was eventually taken over in 1974 by Paccar, the 'mother' of Kenworth and Peterbilt, and closed down soon afterwards. The president had left by then to run the CCC truck firm.

Another Canadian marque that proved itself for many years in the heavy transport sector was Pacific. This company was founded in 1947 by three ex-Hayes employees, but had to cease production in 1991 following a dramatic drop in sales in its specialised sector. Well known American truck companies like Ford, GMC, International, Kenworth and Mack have had their own factories in Canada for

To facilitate the transport of troops and materials to the far north the Alaska Highway was built in record time.

When America entered the war, American troops and trucks spread out over the world. Here we see a convoy of White and GMC trucks in the North African desert.

General Motors built 854,000 trucks and amphibious carriers during World War II. In the civilian sector the MU/MV cab-over-engine model was popular. The cattle trailer was made by Wilson, 1943.

years, in most cases building trucks more suited for the extreme conditions that can be found in Canada.

On the American market 1,376,155 trucks and buses were sold in 1948. Chevrolet, Ford and International had the largest share and were followed by Dodge, Studebaker and GMC.

Naturally the companies producing heavy trucks were lower on the list of sales, for instance Autocar with 2770 trucks, Brockway with 2958, Diamond T with 10,657, Federal with 4026, Mack with 9795 and White with 11,603.

In the light commercial vehicles category we find names such as Crosley, Divco, Hudson and Willys.

We should also remember other heavy trucks that are no longer produced: Biederman, Reo, Marmon-Herrington, Sterling and Ward LaFrance are all still respected for the service they did in the last war and afterwards. Many European transport companies have fond memories of these and other marques used by the armed forces. In fact ex-US Army trucks formed the backbone of the successful international road transport system of today.

When the Germans invaded their neighbouring countries in 1940 growth in the transport sector in these areas came to a grinding halt. For example, of approximately 55,000 trucks in Holland at the time, many thousands disappeared in the war years and the import of new trucks was non-existent for five years. American trucks were especially popular with the German occupying forces and many vanished across the border to be employed on the Eastern front. The robust construction, simplicity and reliability of Diamond Ts, Fords, GMCs, Whites, etc, had already been proved in hard civilian use in the

After the war many ex-US Army trucks were converted for civilian use. This Commer-cabbed Mack truck had a Leyland diesel engine and was built for some years in Great Britain.

'This war eats rolling equipment', proclaims this 1944 Trailmobile advertisement.

Thirties and because they were fitted with powerful engines American trucks were also suitable for running on less efficient alternative fuels. For civilian purposes many were converted to gas generators fuelled by anthracite, coal, coke, wood or peat. For the drivers it was a switch to a smelly and dirty fuel, but at least they were still on the road.

European importers of American trucks, like Beers and Albatros in Holland, had a hard time during the war. In 1940 six new White trucks, still loaded on board a ship of the Holland-America Line, were lost during the bombardment of Rotterdam. Before the war Beers had sold 1706 Diamond T truck and bus chassis, but after war was declared everything came to a standstill. In May 1940 they still had 60 Diamond T chassis on order, but none were delivered to Holland. Those that were underway were delivered to England, and the rest remained in America. During the occupation some importers however managed to hide a number of new American trucks and a lot of spare parts from the Germans by burying them in a peat marsh or underneath hay stacks. After the liberation they were sold as new because they had been perfectly conserved. Many importers also modified existing vehicles to

run on gas. They did everything to keep in business during the war years until the first army surplus trucks arrived on the market in 1945.

In Europe supplies of American vehicles were restored after the war, and to start with thousands of ex-US Army jeeps, trucks, tractors, half-tracks and scout cars were purchased for civilian use and modified accordingly. Dealers in Belgium, Denmark, England, France, Germany, Holland, Italy and elsewhere were assigned to distribute the available trucks among civilian operators.

Large numbers of heavy Diamond T 6x4 and 6x6 trucks, International 542s, Mack NR and NO Models, the famous GMC 6x6 2.5-ton chassis, Autocars, Chevrolets, Dodges and Fargos, FWDs and Canadian Fords, Reos, Whites and many others were all helping to relieve the postwar burden. With the US Army surplus trucks the international transport system was built up again in no time. Major line haul carrier Van Gend & Loos in Holland, for example, was one of the first to run heavy ex-army Mack truck and trailer outfits to Austria and Czechoslovakia. Thousands of tons of goods supplied under the Marshall Aid plan were distributed by the Dutch further into Europe. The army surplus trucks were

Only a few hundred of the chain-driven big Mack FP models were produced between 1940 and 1942. This beautifully restored example is in Ontario, Canada.

Diamond T always built attractive trucks. This heavy 1944 Model 806 with integral sleeper and Brown trailer had a 150HP HB-600 Cummins diesel engine.

During the war no less than 2,600,887 trucks and 529,647 trailers were built in the States and Canada. Ward LaFrance played their part and this 1945 conventional still resembles the wartime models.

slow and heavy, but they had an enormous freight capacity.

Because deliveries of new trucks were slow to get under way, transport companies looked for ways to make army surplus trucks more economical and roadworthy. Dutch Diamond T importer Beers had built up good contacts with Sweden and in 1949 offered the heavy 8-ton Diamond T ex-US Army chassis as an 'economical' 3-tonner. This was achieved by removing one of the two rear axles and fitting a new 90HP Scania-Vabis diesel engine.

The first really new Diamond T chassis was produced in the States in 1947, but without the advantage of military orders the demand was small and prices too high. Besides, this model was fitted with a petrol engine and there was hardly a market for it in Europe due to the ever rising price of fuel.

Mack dealers in Europe also offered modified ex-army units for civilian use way on into the Fifties. NR Series Macks were modified to a 4x2 drive configuration and fitted with the 135HP 6-cylinder Mack Lanova engine. These proved popular trucks for many reborn hauliers. In France haulage company Transports Loheac modified several hundred International H542 tractors, mainly for their own use, and their descendants with modern diesel engines are still widely used. For some time Mack NR models were also remanufactured for civilian

use in Austria by Steyr Daimler Puch. And even in Germany the famous Henschel & Sohn company offered to local hauliers in 1949 the GMC 2.5- to 5-ton ex-US Army truck fitted with their own diesel engine.

Many dozens of European importers were

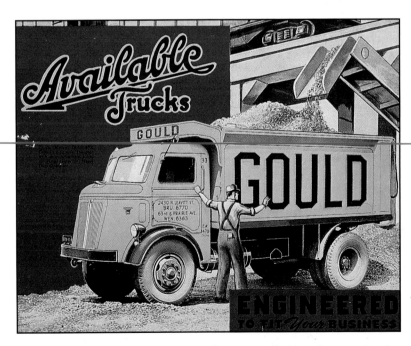

In 1945 the Available range consisted of ten types of COE and conventional trucks. They were fitted with Waukesha gasoline or Cummins diesel engines.

Another robust
looking truck of the
mid-Forties. This
Brockway 260XW
dwarfs its small dairy
trailer.

Mack built the LJT model from 1940 to 1956. It was a magnificent long-haul truck (appropriately in this case bearing the livery of Long Transportation) and was fitted with a Cummings diesel.

After the war hundreds of army surplus trucks stayed behind in Europe. This sturdy Diamond T pulled two trailers full of Marshall Aid goods all the way from Holland to Czechoslovakia.

involved in modifying army surplus vehicles for at least ten to twenty years. Examples include MOL, Terberg, Gina, Labourier, Astra and Mack Trucks (Great Britain) Ltd.

Others had resumed the import of new vehicles from America as soon as they became available. For example the new White WA and WB models looked good in the eyes of Belgian, Dutch and Danish operators, but they lacked a good diesel engine.

Corbitt bought a few eight-cylinder Gardner diesels from Britain, though the most widely used British engine in US chassis became the competitively priced Perkins. In

A Dutch body builder made a good-looking refrigerated truck out of this ex-military GMC 2.5-tonner. An air-cooled Deutz diesel was fitted in place of the standard gas guzzler.

A fine large Belgian truck based on a US Army Mack NR. The stylish refrigerated body and trailer were built by Ackermann (later part of Fruehauf) in Germany.

After the war Mack designed attractive high-quality trucks. Here we have a contemporary brochure cover.

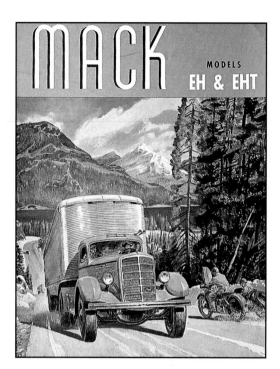

1957 Cummins started a manor diesel engine factory in Scotland as its first venture outside America.

Cummins engines were still not for sale in this part of the world and the diesel engines Hercules offered at the time proved to be unreliable, as did the Danish Bur-Wain that was tried in White chassis around 1947-1948.

In postwar Europe, American trucks with petrol engines were at a disadvantage. Imports were still limited and sales of trucks from across the Atlantic remained low. In the following decade the American manufacturers found out that they had lost the battle for a place in a formerly very lucrative export market.

Peterbilt built one truck per day in 1945. This is a Model 334 in Oregon.

In 1938 Thermo King devised the first mechanically-driven refrigeration system. In the Forties the units were moved from underfloor to the front of the trailer, as this Federal shows.

American trucks were also popular in Belgium. In 1946 several new models came on the market, like this heavy International KB-8.

From 1941 onwards over one million trucks were built yearly in the United States, and though the roads had improved, they were often still far from perfect.

In the Forties Peterbilt built this extra heavy duty model 380 specially for the logging industry.

Available of Chicago built 2500 trucks mostly for local customers in their 47 years of existence.

In 1948 the White Motor Company produced 11,603 trucks of all sizes and shapes, such as this White Super Power oilfield truck.

Kenworth was a pure West Coast truck for a long time and its sturdy conventionals were ideal for forestry work. This heavy Model 888 had a 200HP Cummins NHB-600 diesel.

To comply with the legislation in the West, Mack designed the LTSW longnose in 1946. This model was usually fitted with a 196HP Mack Thermodyne diesel engine, but if more power was required a 400HP Hall-Scott butane or gasoline engine was an option.

The case for heavy-duty trucks

◀ In 1948 Autocar produced 2770 trucks and was one of the smaller builders, but they made a wide range of good quality trucks.

▲ This locally-bodied Diamond T S-type with 6-cylinder gasoline engine was purchased in 1948 by a Dutch customer.

MODEL W-3042-L
GVW RATING 30,000 POUNDS

INTERNATIONAL

DIAMOND T
EXTRA-HEAVY-DUTY MODEL 910N

Nominal Rating 7½ - 10 Tons   Maximum Gross Vehicle Weight 36,000 lbs.
Maximum Gross Weight Six-Wheel Models 40 - 50,000 lbs.
Max. Gross Train Weight 60,000 lbs.   Max. Gr. Tr. Weight Six-Wheelers 76,000 lbs.

General Specifications

AXLE, FRONT: Extra-heavy, I-beam section.
AXLE, REAR, (Timken U-200-P): Extra-heavy full-floating dual reduction axle. Heavy one-piece malleable housing, with inserted sleeves of alloy steel. New design with hypoid bevel gear and pinion in first reduction with second reduction through helical spur gears provides increased load and torque capacity with greater clearance. Axle ratios 5.91 to 1, 6.51 to 1, 7.08 to 1, 7.75 to 1 and 8.69 to 1.
AXLE, REAR, TWO-SPEED (Timken U-300-P): Double reduction two-speed axle, specifications all same as standard Timken U-200-P, but with two sets of helical gears in final

drive permitting choice of axle ratios and vehicle speeds, but is not supplied when two-speed axle is specified. Tractor can be furnished in 154½" wheelbase accordingly.
Auxiliary transmission is standard with single-speed axle.
AXLE, REAR, TWO-SPEED — TRACTOR SERVICE ONLY, (Timken R-300-P): Double reduction two-speed axle, similar to Timken U-300-P, but lighter and of less load capacity. Air shift. Approved for tractor service on paved highways and preferred for this service on account of its lighter weight. Ratios 4.92 to 1 and 6.42 to 1. Auxiliary transmission not supplied with this axle.

◀ The robust W series conventional was International's answer for Western operators in 1948. 2 versions: Cummins diesel or Hall-Scott gasoline or butane engines.

▲ Diamond T wasn't trailing far behind and designed this heavy 910N model with NHB-600 Cummins diesel and a 5-speed Spicer gearbox.

General Motors built the A series GMC for use on the West Coast in 1948. This fine example with Weber trailer is powered by a 238HP 6-cylinder GM diesel engine.

The German truck building industy had to start from scratch after the war. In 1949 Henschel & Sohn was still converting army surplus GMCs for civilian use.

A Peterbilt conventional and Kenworth 'Bullnose' grain hauler from the Forties, photographed in Seattle in 1958.

In 1948 this good-looking Federal Model 29M removal truck, fitted with a 6-cylinder gasoline engine, was sold to a grateful European customer.

After the war export sales of White trucks picked up again with models like the WB-20. This Dutch truck with locally-made cab had a gauge of only 2.20 metres for operation on narrow roads, around 1950.

A beautifully rebuilt Sterling chain-drive truck of 1950 vintage.

The Freightliner COE truck was initially only used by Consolidated Freightlines, who designed and built it, but was also sold to other operators from 1948 onwards.

FROM THE FIFTIES TO THE SEVENTIES

After regularly exceeding one million sales per year, as noted earlier, the commercial vehicle industry in America finally topped 1.5 million in 1964. In the first years after the war approximately seven million people earned a living in the truck building industry and the trucking business. In the mid-Sixties this number had risen to eight million people. Statistics for 1963 show that there were more than 13 million commercial vehicles in use in the States and this figure had reached almost 18 million at the end of the decade. This enormous fleet was used for all types of transport, from mail service to the transport of boats. In the Rock & Roll age and the following Flower-Power era, trucks and buses were taking more and more transport away from the railroads. To get road transport organized, in particular the long-haul services, the federal government had decided in 1952 to reserve more money to build up the Interstate highway network. In 1954 $575

In 1950 Kenworth sold more than 1700 heavy Cummins-powered 6x6 oilfield trucks to Aramco in Saudi

The White Super Power WC series had distinctive styling. This handsome sleepercab tractor with aluminium Trailmobile reefer-semi is bound to have turned some heads.

This gleaming International R-170 with coachbuilt cab and flat deck was working in Europe in 1950.

million and in 1956 $ 1,050 million had been spent on road construction.

Privately financed toll roads like the New York Thruway and the Pennsylvania Turnpike were also encouraged. Even today these and other toll roads in the East form a very important link in the busy flow of intercity traffic.

Line haul carriers have been making good use of the liberal train weights and maximum measurements that apply to these roads. It is permitted to operate a 100-foot combination consisting of two double tandem trailers on specified highways. Special transfer points where trailers can be exchanged have been built, and it goes without saying that this means of transport is very economical. Because these roads are reasonably flat, normal tandem-drive tractors such as the GMC Brigadier or White WG with 'only' 350HP under the hood are proving sufficient to pull two big trailers.

What we now regard as marginal power was a lot 40 years ago. To comply with the minimum speed of 20mph on the highways at the time, truck manufacturers had to fit their trucks with more powerful engines. Twenty years later, in the Sixties, Brockway, International, Mack and White were able to

A typical West Coast truck of the Fifties is this Kenworth Model 523 COE with cattle trailer in Colorado.

Good-looking 1951
Mack LJ with single-
axled Fruehauf trailer.

offer a Turnpike Special that was powered by a
325HP Cummins diesel. It was a relatively
small market, but the manufacturers thought
these models would give them extra prestige
and hence some other sales too.

Although enormous amounts of money
have been spent on the national road network
since the Fifties, a number of Interstate
highways, and even some of the major toll
roads, were and still are in a deplorable state.

This 1951 'needle nose'
Kenworth was still in
use in 1992. The owner
replaced the original
engine with a 400HP
Cummins diesel.

In the early Fifties a Dutch body builder made this streamlined van on a gasoline-powered Chevrolet chassis.

The 1950 truck show in Amsterdam. White importer Albatros showed the first 3000 model that ever rolled off the American production line and the truck was purchased by Bols. Beyond it are Scottish Albion chassis.

A unique streamlined combination based on a Ford F8 in California around 1950.

Holes two feet wide and six inches deep are not a rarity in the concrete road surface in some places. In states like New York, Pennsylvania, New Jersey or Michigan you sometimes have to slalom to avoid potholes on the highway.

The 1956 plan to extend the network of Interstate highways to a total length of 45,000 miles is now almost complete, but the roads need more maintenance than the billions of dollars that motorists pay in road tax seem to be able to pay for.

Despite this enormous problem with the infrastructure, life for a trucker has become a lot more bearable, and the driving qualities and comfort of the American truck have improved enormously over recent years, so bad roads are more of a problem for motorcars than heavy trucks.

With the newly created industrial estates in the East as well as the West, demand for efficient road transport became stronger in the Fifties. Trucks and buses not only had to transport heavier loads, they had to do it faster and more economically.

Brown trucks were designed, like Freightliner, by a transport company, in this case Horton Motor Lines. This rare COE dates from 1952, a year before the firm ceased production.

In 1951 demand for Freightliner trucks became so great that a sales and servicing agreement was made with the White Motor Company. From then on the trucks were called White-Freightliner.

The experience that truck manufacturing companies had gained around the world with heavy army trucks during wartime was put to use for civilian purposes, and when road transport became more important than rail transport, competition amongst the transport companies grew. The demand for powerful trucks that could carry ever heavier loads and still comply with the local regulations rose too.

Production of COE trucks increased and new models were introduced as fast as possible. White launched its famous Model 3000 COE in 1949. It is worth mentioning that the very first truck of this type to roll off the production line in Cleveland, Ohio, was sold to distiller Bols in Amsterdam, Holland.

Mack, on the other hand, announced in 1950 that its 'Traffic Type' COE was no longer in production, but in 1953 returned to this market segment with the H-Series 'cabover'.

In the same year the now classic and, according to some, finest Mack of all time, was launched: the B-Model. Of the most popular types, the B-42 and B-61, respectively 19,729 and 47,459 were built before 1966. Other trucks that sold well in this period were the GMC 500-900 series, the conventional R and DCO cabover line from International, Reo's E series, the White 9000, the Chevrolet 60-80 series and from 1957 onwards Ford's C-series 'low profile cabovers'. The latter has only recently been taken out of production, and passed the Mack AC Bulldog and maybe even Ford's own Model T in the list of best-sellers. Between 1957 and 1962 Mack fitted the same low cab on the N series, as did FWD later for a few of its models.

To comply with the rules on maximum length some truck manufacturers designed a 96-inch BBC cabover (BBC stands for Bumper to Back of Cab).

In the West, truck producers were trying hard to better adapt their products for operating in tough mountain conditions. The lightweight Freightliner COE, designed by Consolidated Freightways just before the war, became available to rivals in 1950.

The Hyster Company from Oregon purchased a Freightliner tandem-drive tractor with a lot of extras fitted. It had a large sleeping compartment, a 10-speed gearbox, an

This 1952 Kenworth conventional with refrigerated trailer is a real classic. The sleeper is still a bit on the small side but the truck has a lot of extras.

A nice picture from the early Fifties showing a Reo E22 or E23 model resting at a Mobil truckstop in Chicago.

adjustable Bostrom driver's seat, a tachometer and electrically operated 'sanders' for traction on slippery surfaces. Mainly built of aluminium, it had travelled four million miles before the current Freightliner Corporation bought it back in 1976. This Freightliner has now been restored and can be admired in the transport sector of the famous Smithsonian Museum in Washington DC.

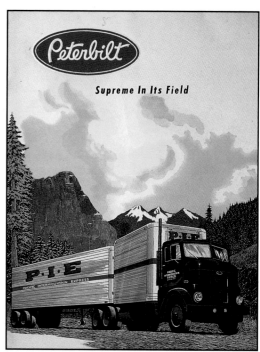

In 1950 Peterbilt introduced the new 350 COE line. In cooperation with P.I.E. some rigs were fitted with a 'dromedary-box' behind the cab.

Very few TE series Sterling COEs were made. This 1950 model could be had with 6-cylinder diesels with outputs ranging from 200 to 300HP.

The name Peterbilt is synonymous with quality and longevity. This model 351 was built in 1953 and was still operational in 1992 hauling cattle in Oklahoma.

When the demand for Freightliner trucks became so great that the small group of enthusiastic engineers in Portland couldn't cope any more, a joint venture was started with the White Motor Corporation in 1951. A year later the Sterling company was taken over by White and in 1953 it was Autocar's turn. Unfortunately the Sterling marque disappeared relatively quickly and though Autocar still exists in name, the real enthusiasts say that the Volvo-GM built Autocar is something completely different to the good old truck that was built in Pennsylvania.

The service and marketing joint venture between White and Freightliner only lasted until 1977. To that date these typical West Coast trucks were sold under the name White-Freightliner.

Since 1982 Freightliner has found a new partner and is now part of the giant Daimler-Benz concern. The other major 'Western' truck manufacturers, Peterbilt and Kenworth, were taken over by Paccar in 1950.

In the same year Kenworth engineers fitted a 175HP Boeing gas-turbine engine in a 10-ton truck. In later years more trucks from Ford, General Motors, International, Mack and Peterbilt would appear with gas-turbines, but they never entered series production due to excessive fuel consumption and lack of instantaneous throttle response. In an effort to gain the attention of potential customers, Peterbilt in 1975 even published a brochure with a gramophone record of gas-turbine engine noise!

As it was, the diesel still had lots of scope for improvement. In the Thirties and Forties many transport companies in the USA experimented with diesel engines to find out if they really were more reliable and

In May 1951 White sold 1170 trucks and Ford 23,261. The big difference is because the light truck market was so much larger than the specialised heavy end.

In Europe, Ford had the largest market share up to the Sixties. This Netam (Fruehauf) built tanker pulled by a C-750 cabover was powered by a 155HP V8 gasoline engine.

economical than gasoline engines. Even though the diesel engine had proved itself in the trucks and buses of independent truckers and small fleets, a lot of large transport companies still preferred gasoline engines.

In 1948, 1,035,174 trucks were sold in America. Of this enormous quantity only 4485 were fitted with diesel engines! In 1950 the number of diesel engined trucks had risen to 12,682, but this was still only 1.3% of all truck sales, and was virtually negligible.

If you look through magazines of those days you will see that the main disadvantage of a diesel was said to be the thick black smoke and noise emitted when the engine

was working hard. But improvements were on the way.

The longevity and potential of, for instance, the HA- and NH-series Cummins diesel and the General Motors two-stroke units proved that there was a market for them in heavy trucking. Although GM had a lot of success with their first 4.71 engine and also with the later 6V-71, GMC still hung on to gasoline engines as standard. In 1960 a truck was introduced with a 275HP 12-cylinder Twin-Six gasoline engine. Rumours have it that this truck could out-run the fastest police car in Canada! All they needed was an extra trailer to store the fuel for this 12-cylinder gas guzzling monster...

On the West Coast large gasoline engines of up to 400HP were built by Buda, Hall-Scott and Hercules, and were possibly even more popular there than in the East.

Because Arizona, California, Nevada, Utah, Oregon and Washington state permitted much greater GVW than other states, large gasoline engines could still be used. The word is that these trucks were unbeatable in the mountains and on the highways, but in the Eighties the popularity of the gasoline engine started to fade as the price of fuel soared. Another type of fuel had been introduced in 1952, when Reo and International fitted their new line of trucks with LPG engines (Liquid Petroleum Gas). A number of these trucks were imported into Belgium, Denmark and Holland.

Corbitt had built up a good reputation during the war. From 1946 onwards they sold approximately 600 trucks per year. Shown is a 1952-54 model.

Other important developments of the Fifties were the 10-speed Fuller 'Road Ranger' gearbox with single stick shift, and a new pneumatic suspension system devised by Neway. Tubeless truck tyres were introduced in 1955, and a few years later Bostrom developed the air-sprung driver's seat. In the Sixties Cummins designed the famous 'Jake Brake' engine brake system and Caterpillar started selling their 1673 diesel engine for trucks. This was the predecessor to the now popular 3406 engine. The oil crisis that hit the world in 1974 accelerated the further improvement of truck diesel engines and turbo-charging became common. Demand for more streamlined trucks also became stronger as fuel prices went up. In the Sixties a lot of the heavy trucks that had been introduced were, to say the least, of angular design, despite the fact that in earlier years there had been some interesting aerodynamic designs.

A good example is the 1954 GMC 950 COE. This popular truck with its high, round snout was followed up in 1964 by the D-series COE, which received the nickname 'Cracker Box' because that is exactly what it looked like. Nonetheless this model sold well and it was twelve years before GMC came up with a new design, the familiar Astro 95, that looked a lot more modern.

Some of the American makes of this period found their way abroad too, but because of the expense of modifying these trucks to European standards and differing legislation, this generation of US-built trucks never matched the success of earlier ones. For

example in America you did not need brakes on the front wheels of some heavy multiwheelers, something that was unthinkable in Europe (apart from on some British eight-wheelers). Yet a new law was passed around the same time in the States placing such high demands on the braking systems of heavy trucks that the local industry was unable to comply. This '121' law stated, amongst other things, that trailers should be fitted with an anti-lock braking system. After years of lawsuits the government had to amend its requirements in 1975 and the rules became slightly less harsh.

Unfortunately the export of American trucks fell back during the Fifties and Sixties,

The Diamond T 921N with 335HP supercharged Cummins diesel engine and integral sleepercab made a great long-haul truck in 1953.

A fleet of well-kept Peterbilt, White and Mack refrigerated trucks photographed somewhere on the West Coast in December 1953.

In 1953 GMC built a wide range types of commercial vehicles. Many were powered by gasoline engines, like this heavy 620 series.

To haul more freight within a length of 60 feet, Freightliner designed a special model in 1953 sporting a topsleeper and a Cummins diesel engine under the floor.

Lucas Bols of Amsterdam, who had been faithful White customers for more than thirty years, purchased a number of Model 3000s for the distribution of alcolholic drinks during the 1950s, having earlier purchased a few WB and WC models. White must have been proud of this particular export order, because even in America the Dutch trucks were pictured in advertisements!

When the market situation changed for the worse the import of heavy trucks from the States nearly came to a halt, and in 1962 the last White WB models were delivered in Belgium, Denmark and Holland. Diamond T trucks weren't doing much better: before the war they were ten a penny, but after the war

not only because of technical and legislative reasons, but also due to a floating dollar rate and the lack of service outlets. Only a few importers in Europe managed to keep on selling US-built heavy vehicles, and then only in small numbers.

For some time in the Fifties and early Sixties gasoline powered models from Chevrolet, Dodge, Ford and GMC were popular in Europe among light to medium-duty truck operators, but heavier models had little chance of competing with the local diesel offerings.

they were a rare sight. Dutch assembler Beers had switched to importing Scania-Vabis. These were fitted with reliable and economical diesel engines and the Swedish quality products quickly ousted the expensive Diamond T gasoline engined trucks.

In 1954 Beers made an effort to market a Diamond T chassis fitted with a 5.65-litre 6-cylinder Scania-Vabis diesel engine. This model SX had a Dutch built cab and attempted to put the best of two worlds together, but because the dollar became stronger the project never got off the ground and spelt the end of the marque in Holland. A few years later another importer tried to get the Diamond T name back on the market but

The Clipper COE was a new Hayes product in 1954. Through the ties the firm had with Great Britain, this truck could be had with a 6-cylinder 275HP Rolls-Royce diesel engine.

A 1954 GMC 950 series COE with matching Great Dane refrigerated trailer in Canada. A similar rig played the leading role in the popular *Cannonball* TV series in the Fifties.

In 1952 Kenworth delivered more than 1000 trucks for the first time. Amongst its custom-built trucks was this strange twinsteer combination for P.I.E. powered by an underfloor Cummins diesel engine.

did not succeed. In 1967 Diamond T joined forces with Reo and lost its independence. The resulting joint venture worked until 1974, then Diamond-Reo Trucks got into difficulties too. Nowadays we can still find the Diamond emblem on the products of Osterlund of Pennsylvania, but these assembled trucks have little to do with the proud old Diamond T product.

Apart from the two above-mentioned names a good number of other US-built trucks, some light-duty, others a bit heavier, were imported into Europe at the time. Among them were such famous names as

Brockway, Chevrolet, DeSoto, Dodge, Fargo, Federal, Ford, GMC, International, Mack, Reo and Studebaker. But none were as successful as in the years before the war or even the Fifties.

Some makes that became known during World War II disappeared again in the Fifties and Sixties. These included Autocar, whose trucks were assembled by Kromhout in Holland for a decade or so. Others were to follow and, apart from the smaller Chevrolet, Dodge, Ford and the like trucks, only Mack really survived in Western Europe. This is mainly thanks to assemblers like Floor in

Because of legislation on the West Coast, lightweight trucks were very popular. This high International RDFC-405 with Brown trailer is built mainly of aluminium.

In 1954 $575 million were spent on improvements to America's roads.

Reo Model 220 with Gold Comet 6-cylinder or V8 petrol engine, 1955.

Hendrickson only produced 60 - 100 trucks per year in the Fifties, and very few of this COE model with International cab.

Holland and Camions Bernard in France, which latter firm was taken over by Mack in 1963, but collapsed three years later. Floor was originally a transport company that also built trailers, but in 1955 they acquired the sole rights for assembling Mack trucks in the Benelux countries. Within a short time hundreds of locally cabbed B Model Macks were put on the road, and the Mack N Series COE was imported fully built-up as well. They found their way to several local- and long-haul operators, until in 1963 the new F Series Mack took their place.

Floor wanted to assemble this new Mack for the European market and built a completely new factory for it, but Mack Trucks decided otherwise and organised their own import via France. This meant a break with the Dutch, and to stay in business the Floor brothers developed their own truck, the FTF heavy-duty COE line, which is still in production. The first models were built up out of remaining spare-parts from the Mack inventory, but later they switched to other American components, such as Detroit Diesel engines and Allison and Fuller gearboxes.

In the meantime things became quiet for Mack in Europe, but from 1974 onwards other

On special request Kenworth designed a small series of CBE (cab-beside-engine) trucks in 1953. They had the advantage that the driver could see more of the road in mountain country. The truck in the picture was built for use in Alaska.

▶ Autocar became part of the White Motor Co. in 1953, and a year later a new factory opened in Exton, Pennsylvania. Apart from many highway and construction chassis, heavy trucks for the logging industry were built.

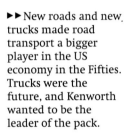

▶▶ New roads and new trucks made road transport a bigger player in the US economy in the Fifties. Trucks were the future, and Kenworth wanted to be the leader of the pack.

In the mountainous states of the West, butane, propane or gasoline engines were long preferred. That's why Kenworth was still offering Buda, Hall-Scott and Hercules engines alongside diesels in 1954.

importers went to great efforts to get the marque back on the road. The economical F700 and the robust DM600 were introduced, becoming reasonably successful, notably in Belgium, England, France, Greece, Holland, Spain and Switzerland. Mack even developed the FM786 series with setback front axle and raised roof in the 1980s to try and clinch a bigger share of the European heavy truck market. During this period White had arranged imports through local companies in some of these European countries too, but most of these American efforts were to no avail.

At home production and sales were substantially better. There were even total yearly truck outputs of over two million ! And despite the fact that more of the well-known names of the pioneer era had folded, like Brockway, Diamond T, Federal, Hayes, Reo, Sterling and others, the remaining truck producers showed a remarkable confidence in the future.

Due to bridge formulas (a combination of axle weight, spread and length) in the West, Budweiser used this type of stretched rig. This is a Reo AC series with an ultra-short cab.

An International RDF-405 Western powered by a 356HP Hall-Scott 10.9-litre butane engine. Models like this were built in the International factory at Emeryville, California.

To meet the
requirements of
certain clients Mack
designed the B-70
series in the Fifties. It
had the front styling of
the 1953 B model, but
the cab of the old L
series.

The 1954 Diamond T
921-C cabover could be
fitted with five
different types of
Cummins diesel
engine, ranging from
190 to 300HP, and
Fuller or Spicer
transmissions.

White's modern COE series with tilted cab was extended by the 6x2 model 3022. You could choose from a 215HP White Mustang gasoline engine or a Cummins NH diesel.

Between 1953 and 1966 Mack produced about 13,000 H60 series cabovers. In the course of time the exterior design changed twice: the first version gained the nick-name 'cherrypicker' and the final model was recognizable by a twin headlight arrangement.

This Leyland Canada model was built in Ontario in 1956-57. As a source of power the Leyland Power Plus 680 diesel was chosen, with International cab, a 5-speed Spicer gearbox and an Eaton 3-speed rear axle. Apart from the engine this truck was totally North American in concept and construction.

Around 1954 Kenworth introduced the replacement for the famous 'Bullnose'. The new 522 model had a lot in common with the later K-Series COE truck.

In the Fifties the International R and V models were popular with large transport companies. Nowadays Roadway has 37,500 trucks in service and is one of the largest transport companies in the States.

The GMC FW-620 COE could be equipped with optional extras such as a luxury driver's seat with head and arm rests, air conditioning, tinted windows and a synchromesh transmission.

In 1956 plans were unfolded to create a highway network of 43,000 miles. This 1957 photograph gives us a good idea of the roads prior to realisation of that plan.

Large truckstops had not yet been conceived in 1958. The driver of this Diamond T with aluminium Utility trailer made a stop at a local café.

Mack's N series only lasted five years. Apart from the Thermodyne diesel a Magnadyne gasoline engine could be fitted. This smart looking tandem-axle N60 with trailer was sold to a European long-haul operator in 1958.

At the end of the Fifties Freightliner was building about 600 trucks a year. This 1958 model with 75-inch BBC sleeper is pulling a set of Wilson aluminium doubles for the transport of cattle.

The construction of some superhighways made it possible to use rigs with two trailers on the East Coast too. This Mack B 773LST with 335HP Cummins diesel engine and Mack 15-speed transmission pulled a GCW of 62 tons along the New York Thruway.

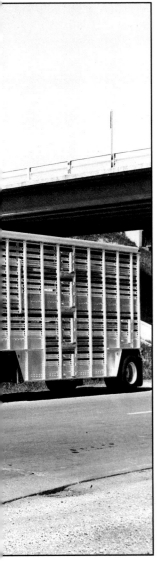

A 100 feet long Autocar with Kentucky tandem trailers. Trucks on the Interstate highways had to be able to climb a 3% gradient at a minimum speed of 20mph in 1959.

Peterbilt became part of the Paccar Group in 1958. This on/off-highway Model 383 with a GCW of 75 tons was used for harvesting sugarcane in Hawaii.

After the takeover of Sterling, Freightliner and Autocar, White managed to get a majority share in Reo Motors Inc. in 1957. Reo continued to produce trucks under its own name until 1967.

Hendricksons were usually sold as on/off-highway trucks. This unusual BD-360 conventional highway tractor with 380HP Caterpillar diesel engine was photographed in Florida in 1959.

In 1958 the International DCO-405 COE formed a welcome addition to the existing IHC range. In the picture we see a fine Mexican refrigerated rig that was still in use in 1989.

One of the rarer trucks from Canada was the Peninsula. In 1961-62 about ten were built and fitted with a choice of Cummins, Detroit or Rolls-Royce diesel engines.

In 1960 GMCs production was 104,310 trucks. The Tiltcab model illustrated with 72" BBC cab was also available as a Chevrolet.

The International DF-400 series of the early Sixties shared cab panels with various COE types. The fiberglass hood was available in three lengths, an easy way to create a new-style conventional.

Mack launched the successful F series in 1962. This F607 with 187HP END673P Thermodyne diesel engine and 10-speed gearbox was used on international hauls in Europe.

Logging has always been one of the most important industries on the West Coast. This 1962 Mack B773LS was still in operation in Washington State in 1985.

A total of 47,459 B61 models were sold, making it Mack's bestseller until then. For many people it is also the most handsome truck Mack ever built. The classic dumptruck in the picture dates from 1962.

From 1960 onwards Oshkosh on/off-highway trucks had a strangely designed front windscreen and roofline to suit rugged conditions.

A 1962 Hayes Clipper conventional in Vancouver, Canada. This truck was powered by a 380HP Cummins diesel engine.

Because of the cube-shaped cab, the 1962 GMC D series COE got the nick name 'Crackerbox'. It became reasonably popular, especially because it was powered by a Detroit diesel engine.

By using aluminium and fiberglass the cab of the White 5000 COE weighed almost a ton less than that of its predecessor. This Trailmobile double bottom outfit dates back to 1963.

Mack's C series was only produced for two years. This 9-axled monster weighed 56 tons and was in use in Michigan in 1963.

An Autocar Model
A75T with Cummins
NH-220 diesel engine
and Fuller 10-speed
gearbox pulling a set
of Fruehauf tankers in
1963.

Brockway became part
of Mack in 1956 but
continued to build its
own trucks. This 1964
Series 400 COE is one
of the later models
fitted with a Mack cab.

Due to its power and durability the Mack B61
revolutionized the Australian transport scene.
Here it is pulling a cattle roadtrain on a lonely
Queensland outback route in 1964.

In 1967 White decided to merge their Diamond T and Reo companies because they were building almost the same models. This beautiful T931C cabover in Michigan was still a 'real' Diamond T.

In 1965 a European operator used this Chevrolet 60-Series Medium Conventional with V8 gasoline engine as a household removal truck.

In the Sixties Oshkosh designed a number of these colossal D-Series 12x10 14 cubic yard capacity concrete trucks. They were powered by a 350HP Caterpillar diesel engine and grossed 48 tons.

In 1965 The Mack B model was followed up by the R600/700 series.

In 1967 GMC produced
130,659 trucks. This is
a heavy duty 9500
series conventional,
powered by a 6-7IN GM
diesel engine, hauling
a good load on the
West Coast.

A handsome 1968
Kenworth K100 with
refrigerated trailer in
California. This model
increased Kenworth's
sales fourfold between
1969 and 1970.

In the 30 years of its existence Sicard of Canada only built 2500 trucks, mostly for on/off-highway operators in Quebec. This model was introduced in 1968, shortly before the firm folded. Sicard had built some models of Paccar group trucks and was ultimately absorbed by that firm.

To meet the demand for larger cement transit mixers, FWD designed this multi-axle combination in 1964. It was based on a Model C-88 Tractioneer chassis and had an 8x8 drive arrangement.

Hayes' last highway truck was the Clipper 200. It was a sturdy conventional with distinctive looks. Under the fiberglass hood lurked the standard Cummins NH-200 diesel engine, one of 14 different engine options from 1969.

In the Seventies Kenworth experimented with a number of new designs. This strange semi-forward control model never got past the prototype stage.

In 1972 Hendrickson tried to stimulate sales of highway trucks with two H models, which came with a long or short nose.

Apart from a large number of on/off-highway conventional models, Oshkosh offered the 4x2 and 6x4 E series COE in 1971. This truck was also built for some years in South Africa by Barlows.

Mack DM series trucks were also made with offset cabs for improved visibility, notably on construction sites. Here we see a heavy haulage rig in the port of Rotterdam in 1972.

A 1971 Autocar Model A64B with Dorsey widespread-tandem trailer.

In 1972 International Harvester bought a 33% share in Dutch DAF. The result was the DAF N2500. In fact this was a Paystar with a 250HP DAF diesel engine and a 13-speed Fuller transmission.

Dodge still made heavy trucks in 1973, like the CNT950 Bighorn. Under the impressive hood lies a NTC-350 Cummins diesel engine. This one was operating in California.

From 1953 onwards the Crane Carrier Company, or CCC for short, constructed chassis for the building sector. The picture shows a Century 8x4 truck with a GCW of 32 tons in Canada around 1974.

Just before the company folded Diamond-Reo launched a series of new conventional and COE trucks in 1974. This C-119DB Raider train in Michigan had a 1693TA Caterpillar diesel behind the characteristic grille.

White-Freightliner designed the Powerliner in 1974. It was produced mostly for independent operators and apart from the luxurious cab it had the option of a 600HP Cummins NTC-600 diesel engine.

The Mack Cruise-Liner was mainly intended for West Coast operators. Apart from Mack's own Maxidyne, Maxitorque and Econodyne engines there was the choice of Detroit, Cummins and Caterpillar diesels up to 525HP.

A Ford W-Series COE in California is a rare sight. This Ford with aluminium cab, NTC-290 Cummins diesel engine and 10-speed Spicer transmission never became very popular.

Quite a range of trucks have been built in Canada. Scot entered the market in 1972 with its base in Nova Scotia. This conventional with Caterpillar diesel engine arrived new on the market in 1977.

The very last Hayes to roll off the production line in 1975 was sold to MacMillan-Bloedel. This mighty HDX truck has been in use for 18 years in the wooded hills of Vancouver Island. It was designed to haul weights up to 150 tons.

Alongside the Road Boss conventional White successfully introduced the COE Road Commander in 1978. With engine options up to 450HP it could easily pull a 74-ton bulk train in Michigan.

The designs of the Rubber Railway Company of Ontario were weird to say the least. This 10x6 concrete mixer was powered by a 903 Cummins diesel engine and had a Fuller 8-speed gearbox in 1976.

A very attractive 1978 352 COE Peterbilt car transporter operating in California. It is powered by a 425HP 3406 Caterpillar diesel and had already done over a million miles when this photograph was taken.

The Kenworth LW924 was designed as an on/off-highway truck. This 1978 Canadian-owned rig has been fitted with a 600HP Cummins diesel engine and is used for long-haul refrigerated transport.

At the end of the Seventies a number of heavy duty Autocar DC-7366S 6x6 drive chassis with 250HP Caterpillar 3306T diesel engines were exported to Europe.

The heavy GMC conventional of 1978 was called the General, while the similar Chevrolet series was badged Bison.

In an effort to give the COE trucks more esteem among independent truckers, GM launched the Titan SS, which sported a modified cab and a powerful 420HP Detroit Diesel engine.

As the computer age dawned there were 20 million trucks on US roads.

THE EIGHTIES AND NINETIES

The Sixties and Seventies, apart from the oil crisis and the new '121' braking regulations, were relatively quiet for the American truck builders. From 1980 onwards a lot more happened, not only in terms of changes in the transport business, but also in terms of technical developments and the streamlining of heavy trucks.

Nowadays there are no more new highways being constructed, apart from the odd ring road around a city, and the construction costs have risen enormously. The estimates today state that one new mile of Interstate highway out of town costs over four million dollars and in urban districts almost twenty million dollars.

Because the capacity of some important through-routes is already too small for the volume of traffic, plans need to be made to come up with a number of new 'super-highways'. In this respect the government has recently been studying the possibility of constructing a second Interstate 80 road from East to West straight across the continent, but the gigantic cost, to say nothing of objections from hundreds of environmentalists, will

Since 1954 the Canadian Kenworth Company in British Columbia has fabricated special models for the local market. Premay in Alberta uses this mighty 849S for work in the oilfields.

In 1980 Dean Hobbensiefken in Oregon launched an improved version of his futuristic Paymaster. The truck has a Detroit Diesel - Spicer/Rockwell driveline placed midships which can be removed in-unit for servicing.

Every road haulage company and the railroads tried to do the job for the lowest possible price, and the competition was intense. Anybody who had some money could buy a truck and start his own transport company.

Then in 1935 President Roosevelt placed road transport under the responsibility of the Interstate Commerce Commission (ICC), following advice from the American Trucking Associations. The Commission took its duties seriously and started checking all transport permits on a national scale. At the same time two other organizations were founded by the ATA: the RCCC and the IRCCC, to coordinate the regular and irregular transport of goods by road.

These organizations still exist, and until recently, the ICC was not very popular among truck owners. Except when you were hauling perishable loads, it was almost impossible to get a transport permit, which was especially tough for newcomers. But in 1980 the power of the ICC diminished. The whole permit system was rewritten and fresh legislation made it possible for many newcomers to start a transport company.

The legislation concerning the maximum length and GVW of heavy trucks was also changed. Although each state still has its own size and weight limitations for trucks, it is

probably delay this project for several more years.

In the Eighties road transport did become regulated. Prior to 1934 there were virtually no rules or regulations for the transport of goods or people by road.

The Peterbilt 359 Conventional with Caterpillar 3406B diesel engine and 9- or 13-speed Fuller gearbox was a favourite amongst independent truckers and small transport companies. This one dates from 1986.

After White was taken over by Volvo in 1982, Western Star became a separate business in Canada. This 1985 model 4942 is equipped with a luxurious 88-inch Double Eagle sleeper.

The Kenworth T600A 'Anteater' was something all new in 1985. Its radical lines were not very popular in the beginning, but more than half of the current Kenworth range now has similar aerodynamic design.

Allthough this 1988 Freightliner FLC Conventional still resembles a truck of the Fifties, the Mercedes-Benz influence has improved technical aspects and driver comfort enormously.

now possible to drive a tractor-semitrailer of 80,000 lbs with a maximum trailer length of 48 feet anywhere on the continent. In the old days the length of the total rig used to be the decisive factor, but since 1982 only the trailer has been limited in length. Trailers with a width of 8½ feet are now also permitted.

Because of the change of legislation, sales of heavy trucks in the Class 7 and 8 segments have also seen some changes. In previous decades just as many COE trucks were sold as conventionals, but now the ratio has changed dramatically. Trucks-with-noses outsell COE trucks three or four to one. Only the large transport companies with fleets of maximum volume trailers are staying faithful to the COE, mostly to standardize their fleets. Smaller companies and independent truckers clearly prefer the conventional. This is partly for engine accessibility and ride comfort but

mostly for its looks, because image is often more important to the American trucker than efficiency or comfort. This also becomes clear in the yearly Unocal inquiry filled in by thousands of professional truckers. In this research fifteen of the newest Class 8 models are tested for popularity among drivers each year. Like elswhere in the world different truckers prefer different trucks, but it appears to be a fact that a Mack trucker is more conservative than the owner of a WhiteGMC.

According to this survey Peterbilt and Kenworth trucks are purchased primarily for their prestige and trade-in value, not for their driving characteristics or economy. However most modern US trucks are fuel-efficient too and provide excellent earning potential.

Although many a truck still has the looks of the Forties, the present generation of 'long noses' built by Peterbilt, Kenworth and

Freightliner have been dramatically updated under the skin. Efficiency and driving quality have improved enormously and the unparallelled longevity has remained unchanged.

However, the old fashioned models, or as the salesmen prefer to say, 'trucks with traditional styling', are still somewhat cramped in the cab. Even the influence of the European mother companies seems to have been forgotten. The new Classic FLD120 and the extra-long nosed Classic XL conventional by Freightliner have been improved considerably in the technical sense, but apart from a few new gauges, a new driver's seat and some smart upholstery, the overall shape of the cab seems to have changed little. The same applies to the Kenworth W900B, the Peterbilt 379, the Western Star 4900, the Marmon 57P and a few more of these large beasts with their long hoods. They look good but are not particularly roomy or modern inside. On the other hand there are plenty of trucks on the road now that are definitely up to date, like the latest generation of streamlined trucks.

Driven by the oil crisis in the Seventies many experiments were carried out to improve the aerodynamics of large trucks. and as a result topspoilers, side fenders and other fibreglass panelling have helped to reduce fuel consumption. This was the first step in a transformation of appearance, but generally the trucks looked the same as twenty years earlier. In 1985 Kenworth was the first to launch a truck that was radically changed: the T600A 'Anteater'. Its streamlined design made it look like a truck in a science-fiction film, and in the beginning few truckers took to it, but as the cost of transport rose demand for this model grew.

The Pacific P500 was new for 1985. In 1947 this firm built its first on/off-highway truck; the last was produced in 1991.

Navistar-International came second in 1993 Class 8 sales with a total of 38,589 trucks. The picture shows a Canadian 9300 with extra-lift steering axle and aluminum dump body.

At the beginning of the Nineties half of total Kenworth production consisted of the aerodynamic T600 and T800 models. Soon after, the equally streamlined T400 and the T450 were introduced for use in the distribution or construction sectors.

Even though these models offer great advantages in fuel economy, driving qualities and comfort, there are still truckers who don't want to drive the new 'plastic' trucks.

For these diehards Kenworth still builds the angular W900B conventional, and this range was broadened recently with the introduction of the W900L, which has an even longer nose. Kenworth still makes a COE, the K100E, too, but there is much more in their line-up. In the Fifties Kenworth sold no less than 1700 ultra-heavy rigs to Aramco for use in the Arabian oilfields. Since then the company has remained the market leader in this sector and monsters like the 848, 850, 993 and Super 953 are still being sold to the oil, mining and lumber industry worldwide. The appearance of these supertrucks has hardly changed over the years, largely because the market for them is limited and development costs gigantic.

We have already seen that Hayes was forced to close its gates in 1975. Perhaps the products of this Canadian company were too good: a working life of twenty years was nothing special, and even now you can still see them in action, along with lots of ancient Kenworths.

In 1991 is was Pacific's turn to go bankrupt. This was another Canadian constructor of super-heavy on/off-highway trucks. Based in Vancouver, Pacific was founded in 1947 and was renowned for colossal trucks intended for the logging and mining industries.

Numbers produced of the last models, the P12 and P16, were reasonable, but not high enough to compensate for the rising cost of production. In 1992 a number of ex-Pacific employees launched a new truck, the Grizzly, a large four-wheel drive pick-up truck with a Cummins B5.9 turbo-diesel engine, designed for support work in the logging, mining and oil industries.

Another recent arrival on the Canadian market is the Challenger, designed in 1987 by transport operator John Casanave. He built the first truck in his backyard and this gigantic monster was the beginning of a successful small enterprise.

The custom-built Challenger is made for the transport of huge logs over unmade roads and is fitted with an all Mack or Cummins/Allison driveline. With power outputs of up to 600HP Challengers are extremely suitable for operation at train weights of more than 100 tons, and are mainly used on Vancouver Island.

The world market for this type of truck is very limited, and other specialists such as Hendrickson, FWD and Oshkosh have had to diversify their activities considerably in the recent past to get through the economic downturn of the Eighties. Apart from heavy trucks, Hendrickson nowadays constructs the HME fire engines, cranes, cement mixers and a range of small trucks.

An interesting recent product is the VT-100 Bullet highway truck, a streamlined conventional that can be fitted with any contemporary engine made by Cummins, Caterpillar or Detroit Diesel – and of course the potential client can choose from a long list of optional extras to suit individual needs.

Not too much is heard nowadays of the once glorious FWD marque. Nevertheless the trucks are still being built in the Clintonville

factory in Wisconsin, fire engines, military trucks, as well as 4x4 and 6x6 drive trucks for municipal services, representing the main output.

Oshkosh is probably the most famous in this series. Having passed the age of 75, this company has broadened the scope of its activities considerably, now producing fire fighting trucks for airports, concrete mixers, snowploughs, all sorts of military trucks, heavy transport trailers, highway trailers and even luxury campers! Oshkosh made a name for itself in the Gulf War with its HEMTT 8x8 tactical trucks, while in the heavy class Oshkosh is undoubtly the most important supplier to the American armed forces.

Latest top truck in the Oshkosh military range is the 'Heavy Equipment Transporter', of which an initial series of 1044 was built for the forces. This 500HP 8x8 M1070 model is coupled to a five-axle semi-lowloader and is capable of transporting a 70-ton battle tank.

Orders from the armed forces often decide the future of a truck manufacturer. Western Star in Canada booked an order in 1991 to build 2750 military trucks. The four-wheel drive LSVW 40.10 is based on an European

The 1987 Freightliner FLD112 is a popular intercity truck. Fitted with the Mercedes LN cab it set new standards of comfort for American truckers.

Iveco design, and this lightweight truck is planned for introduction to the civilian market as well.

Western Star trucks are built in Kelowna, BC, and approximately 3000 Class 8 conventional trucks per year find their way to North American owners.

Western Star developed as an offshoot from the White Motor Company in the early Seventies and was taken over in 1991 by its Australian distributor. Western Star trucks were assembled in Australia for a number of years, but are now imported fully built-up from Canada again.

In 1991 the Canadians made a deal with Dutch truck manufacturer DAF to sell Western Star trucks through their outlets worldwide. For some years DAF also had contacts with International Harvester in the USA. This joint venture produced the heavy DAF N2500 on/off-road conventional, which was in fact an International Paystar 5000 with a DAF diesel engine. IHC's 33% share in DAF Trucks has long since been dissolved, but the

current Navistar-International company still has the Paystar 5000 in its program. Under the impressive hood we nowadays find a 425HP Caterpillar diesel engine and an extra large 8-speed Fuller RTX gearbox, which make the Paystar a popular truck in the on/off-highway sector.

Navistar ranked second in the Class 8 sales list for 1993.

The company's whole range of trucks was redesigned in the late Eighties to appeal more strongly to large truck fleet operators where efficiency, reliability and longevity are the most important factors. At the top of the list we find the 9300 classic conventional and the 9400 aerodynamic version, as well as the 9600 and 9700 COE. The latter incorporates a setback front axle, a Hi-Rise sleeper and more streamlined add-ons.

The new International 9200 with 112-inch BBC cab was introduced in 1992. This is a streamlined model that has some resemblance to the big conventionals, but sports a shorter hood and has a lighter specification. And of

Since the Volvo takeover of White much has changed for the better. In 1993 the company had a market share of 12.3% in the heavy sector. Pictured is the WCM Conventional.

course Navistar still makes a whole range of medium-duty models too, as well as school buses.

Navistar's 9000 Series is still doing well on the COE market. This Class 8 segment has in recent years only totalled around 15,000 units annually. Large line haul carriers like J.B. Hunt, CRST, Schneider and some other well-known names are Navistar's main targets in the COE market, as these firms have regularly purchased one hundred or more International COE tractors at a time.

Freightliner, which has been controlled by Mercedes-Benz since 1982, also builds a COE model that sells well, the FLB Cab-Over-Engine. This is a typical American truck and the basic styling hasn't changed much in forty years, although the exterior look was considerably revised in 1993. But under the skin everything is much more up to date and the current COE Freightliner range, consisting of seven different models, clearly shows some European influences. The American driver will love it because it's well finished, has a modern dashboard, good ventilation and heating

system, excellent seats, lots of usable interior space and above all, the new truck rides much better than older designs from the competition. In general this is also true of other Freightliner models of which some, like the FLC/FLD112 and the lighter 'Business Class' Series, are fitted with a Mercedes cab. New for the construction sector is the FLD120SD with forward axle, a twinsteer FLD 11284SD 8x4 chassis, an FL70/80 6x4 'Baby 8' truck, and some 4x4 and 6x6 drive variants on these offerings. The FL/MB series is fitted with a Cummins or Mercedes diesel engine and falls just short of the heavy Class 8 qualifications, which is why it is called 'Baby 8'.

The call for more comfort and living space in the cab also led Freightliner to design conventionals with integrated sleeping compartments and standing room. For example, the FLD112 or FLD120 conventional for 1994 can be had with a '70 inch Raised Roof Sleeper Cab' or a 'Hi-Style 64 Sleeper Box'. In looks these are similar to the WhiteGMC and Peterbilt offerings in this

After the abolition of a maximum length for tractors in 1982, the market for cabovers like the International 9700 has declined considerably.

respect. They are ideal trucks for long-haul operators driving in shifts, because with so much luxury even the cost of a night in a motel can be saved.

Freightliner celebrated its 50th aniversary in 1992 (even though the first trucks had been made a year or two earlier). This was also the year that all previous production records were broken and Navistar-International was being knocked from its first place in Class 8 sales. As might be expected, a lot has changed in marketing and service under German management, and all for the better, because in 1993 Freightliner topped the charts, producing no less than 48,000 trucks. In the intermediate sector, Class 4-7, Ford is still the largest. It is doing its best to sell more trucks in the prestigious top category and has thrown some significant heavyweights into the ring. The AeroMax 120 for long haul-transport and the robust LTLS-9000 for construction companies were introduced in 1992 and are popular choices, notably in the East and Mid-West. Both models can be fitted with a large number of different diesel engine options, including the new Detroit Diesel Allison Series 60. These 12.7-litre engines, with outputs ranging from 365 to 450HP, are becoming very popular and are fitted with advanced technics such as electronic fuel injection. Naturally they also comply with the stringent 1994 American exhaust emission regulations. Both Cummins and Caterpillar are also producing electronically controlled engines, Cummins having devised the integrated CELECT fuel management system

for its new 460HP N14-460E COMMAND diesel engine and Caterpillar having developed a 425-460HP 3406B engine with PEEC (Programmable Electronic Engine Control) system.

Besides complying with the stiff environmental regulations this new generation of diesel engines has the advantage of being much more economical. As an optional extra an electronic fault-finding system can be fitted, so that maintenance is simplified. Things like that can considerably shorten the standstill time in the service bay. Mack has also fitted its 400HP E7 series diesel engines with a programmable computer system called V-MAC. These electronically assisted engines have been fitted to the standard CH Series since 1992.

Mack Trucks, practically owned by Renault since it bought a major stake in 1978, sold 16,660 Class 8 trucks in 1993. Mack has been struggling for a few years but with modern products, and a much improved economy in the States, better times seem to be here again for one of the world's most famous truck manufacturers. With French aid a good strategic plan has been devised, and by broadening its product range and introducing a new 450HP E7 diesel engine for 1994, Mack continues to pursue its sales growth policy. The all new 'top-of-the-line' CL Series longnose, launched in 1992, has been very well received. It has a 10-inch longer hood than the CH600 and can therefore be fitted with Mack's most powerful E9 diesel engines ranging from 450 to 520HP. Under pressure

A beautiful 1989 Freightliner FLD120 with aluminium Cobra dump semi-trailer in Ontario, Canada. Under the hood sits an electronically managed 425HP 60 series Detroit Diesel.

The Ford LTL-9000 was launched in 1981 as a spin-off from the CLT-9000 COE. This 11 axle 'centipede' transports steel in Michigan.

from Renault Mack also agreed to offer more vendor components. Nowadays a Mack can, as an option, be fitted with a choice of Caterpillar, Cummins or Detroit Diesel engines, as well as Fuller or Spicer gearboxes and Eaton or Rockwell axles. 'Just as the customer wants it', as has been the slogan of many other US truck builders for decades.

Apart from the CL600 for highway operation there is the CL700 for tough on/off highway work. New for the construction sector are the redesigned RD/RM600 and the unusual Mack FDM700 mixer chassis, which was designed in collaboration with Savage, while in the lighter sector Mack introduced the follow-up to the MS Mid-Liner. Also still available are the big Super-Liner conventional (for some markets) and the cabover Ultra-Liner. The RB/DM600 and RD800 on/off-highway models are yet other models in the heavy line-up. The slightly outdated medium-duty MR cabover is due for replacement with a new low cab refuse collection chassis in 1994.

The Allentown Bulldogs have always been very durable trucks, of which many have found worldwide acceptance, and that is enough reason for Renault to support Mack in decades to come.

Another truck building company that owes its existence to a European firm is White. From the moment that Volvo took over the company in 1981 things started to get better for this 94 year old firm. Volvo-GM Heavy Truck Corp., as it is now called, crept up to third place in the Class 8 sales statistics for 1993. Under the name WhiteGMC a broad range of up to date trucks is marketed in the heavy class. In addition, the company still manufactures the legendary Autocar on/off-highway truck, and assembles a number of medium-weight Volvo distribution trucks. Streamlined models are an important part of the Volvo-GM range of today, providing most of the 20,910 sales in the over 15-ton category for 1993. WhiteGMC models with long names like the 'Tall Integral Sleeper Aero ES' have found ready acceptance with many a long-haul operator. Plainly this vehicle has a lot to offer. It is the top of the line in Volvo-GM's aerodynamic range and the 'slippery' conventional offers the driver an unparallelled standard of comfort and roominess. All possible American engine, transmission and rear axles combinations can be had, and it is even available with a sophisticated all-Volvo driveline. In 1992 one third of all WhiteGMC and Autocar chassis sold in Canada were built up of Volvo components.

Volvo is doing its best to integrate European and American know-how in its worldwide products. It isn't coincidental that the new Swedish and Brazilian built Volvo NL conventional looks a lot like its American WhiteGMC brothers. An interesting development that combines the best from Gothenburg and Greensboro is the new Volvo NE conventional. Based on the WhiteGMC WG model and fitted with a complete Volvo driveline, it was introduced in 1992 as a genuine 'world truck concept' for export.

When the Volvo-White Truck Corp. agreed to a joint venture with General Motors in 1986, many people were convinced that names like GMC and Chevrolet would only appear on pick-up trucks and vans from then on.

Nothing could be further from the truth, and although Class 8 models like the General and Astro were phased out several years ago, in 1993 there were still heavy GMC and Chevrolet trucks being built in Michigan.

Since 1970 the model range of both makes had been almost identical. The GMC TopKick and the Chevrolet Kodiak today are good selling trucks in the medium-weight class. Large V8 gasoline engines with electronic injection are still very popular in this sector, but the trucks can also be fitted with a Caterpillar 3116 diesel engine.

Peterbilt Motors Company builds some very attractive trucks, and is synonymous with success for most independent truckers. The company has built gleaming supertrucks for the owner-operator, like the classic Model 379. To survive, Peterbilt started streamlining their models, and the Model 377A/E conventional or the Model 372 COE are good examples. The holding company, Paccar, also owns Kenworth and British Foden and gave Peterbilt access to European know-how. In the new COE model that influence is clearly visible. The cab interior and maintenance aspects have been updated considerably. Like Kenworth, Peterbilt also builds a smaller truck, the Mid-Ranger series, directly derived from a MAN-VW model. It is built in Brazil, just like Ford's Cargo, and shipped to the States.

In 1987 transport operator John Casanave started building the Challenger logging truck in Western Canada. They are built by hand and are powered by a V8 Mack E9 or Cummins KTA 600 diesel engine with power ratings from 400 to 600HP.

Paccar produced 40,500 Class 8 trucks in 1993. The picture shows a beautifully kept W900B conventional with Trailmobile semi-trailer hauling beer in California.

The last and probably most prestigious name in this line-up is Marmon of Texas. This company evolved from the famous Marmon-Herrington Corporation, which in the Thirties and Forties was best known for its indestructible off-highway trucks and 'all-wheel drive' Ford conversions.

Since 1963 Marmon has built exclusive conventional and COE trucks, especially for owner-operators. 70% of its production is sold to this category, and by popular demand Marmon re-introduced the beloved P-model conventional in 1992. This impressive and fully-equipped longnose is built along with the streamlined L-, R- and S-models. Various sized integral sleepers with lots of amenities and a very plush interior (with British sheepskin upholstery) must make even the most pampered owner-operator feel at home in a Marmon truck. And of course the current line of hand-built Marmons is fitted with all the modern technology under the hood. They are far from cheap, but will last almost forever. With recent joint ventures abroad, such as the assembly deal with Trailers de Monterrey in Mexico, the chance of seeing a Marmon outside America is growing. However there is little likelihood that any of the products mentioned above will ever appear in quantity on European soil.

In fact 1993 exports of American trucks, not counting Canada and Mexico, showed a dramatic decline from the numbers sold prior to 1960. Volvo-GM, for example, only sold 796

trucks to the Middle East and South America in 1992. Mack has the best record in this respect and there are 65 countries around the world where the Bulldog is still on sale.

In countries like Australia and New Zealand it is a different story, for here there are still great opportunities for American products.

Mack for one has extensive factories down-under, where specific models are developed to comply with local road transport needs. With a market share of 16.6 percent in 1993 and a range of 20 locally built models in production, Mack Trucks Australia has come a long way since its foundation in 1963. Kenworth and International are also busy building and selling truck models on the other side of the globe which are unknown in America itself. Mainly by setting up local assembly operations rather than importing fully built-up vehicles in this part of the world, US truck builders have been able to keep up or improve

their share of the market, often in the face of tough competition from Japanese, European or local manufacturers.

Most of the trucks directly exported from the USA find their way to South America, the Middle East and Africa. The recent NAFTA trade agreement with Mexico has generated high expectations, for the word is that this market will purchase 10,000 American trucks per year. Volvo-GM, Navistar-International, Freightliner and Marmon have joined up with existing Mexican truck builders and several assembly operations are now already in full swing.

The 'New Europe' with more than 300 million inhabitants ought to be a promising prospect for American trucks, but they are just too expensive, too different and have too little servicing and parts back-up. The modern generation of American trucks may have retained its renowned longevity and robust

Almost 95% of the planned 43,000 miles of Interstate highways have been completed. High costs and objections from environmental groups will probably stop the last 5% being built.

GCWs and weight over the axles are calculated through a complex bridge formula in the West. This 75 foot long Freightliner Dual Steer COE is hauling woodchips in Montana.

In 1991 the Australian importer took over Canadian Western Star Trucks, but production still takes place in Kelowna, British Columbia.

construction, but it is too far removed from European legislation. The 1994 US truck product is certainly just as good as any foreign offering, even in terms of fuel efficiency and creature comforts for the driver, but it is still a breed apart.

Holding companies like Mercedes-Benz, Renault or Volvo don't feel much like bringing American trucks to Europe either, because they would compete directly with their own products.

In 1993 the US Class 8 market was good for 158,000 units, while exports of American-built heavy-duty trucks rose 16 percent. With only 98,730 heavy trucks sold in 1991, the economy has dramatically improved in two years. These figures show that worldwide popularity of American trucks is definitely on the rise again.

In Texas it takes Marmon 21 days to build a truck, but they are hand-built from proprietary components. This is a Lightweight Model 57L.

For really heavy loads Mack has the RD800. It can be ordered with engines up to 500HP and a choice of transmissions.

The Kenworth T800 is
an aerodynamic truck
but without plastic
add-ons. Here we see a
15,000-gallon Westank-
Willock B-train
operating in Canada.

In 1986 Peterbilt replaced the 359 Conventional with the 379. Owner operator Brad Jansen uses this wonderful 40-ton transfer dump to haul sand and gravel in southern California.

The export of American trucks to Europe is virtually non-existent these days. This Mack MH600 Ultra-Liner operating in Holland is an exception.

Friderici in Switzerland is famed for its Kenworth fleet. They own 50 units, including a couple of new K100E Aerodynes.

Wreckers are often beautifully executed. This is a 1989 Peterbilt Model 378 operating in Florida.

In 1990 Kenworth launched an improved version of the T600A with an even more streamlined appearance.

In Canada more than 30% of all Autocar/WhiteGMC sales have a complete Volvo driveline. This Aero ES with integral sleeper is fitted with a 400HP 6-cylinder Volvo VE12 diesel engine.

Freightliner ranked at the top of the sales list in 1993 and sold 48,000 Class 8 trucks. This 64-ton GCW B-train is being pulled by an FLA Raised Roof COE in Nova Scotia.

Another good-looking
truck from Canada:
the bulk tanker was
built by King
Equipment Mfg. and
the tractor is a
Peterbilt Model 377.

The Ford Louisville has
been on the market for
over 20 years but after
the 1991 facelift it still
looks up to date.

Kenworth produced nearly twice as many Class 8 trucks in 1993 as in 1991, but only 10% of these were COEs. Independent trucker Henry Good has done over a million miles in his K100 Aerodyne.

A 1990 Autocar ACM with 425HP Caterpillar diesel engine, Fuller 18-speed gearbox, Rockwell axles and Hendrickson suspension. The 76-ton combination transports lead and zinc ore in Alaska.

The Kenworth 850 is a real giant in the off-highway league. This dumper has a 525HP Cummins KTA525 diesel engine and an Allison automatic transmission.

The majority of Peterbilts sold today are of the streamlined variety, such as this Model 377, available with a forward or setback front axle design.

Kenworth started building trucks in Australia in 1971. The T650 is one of these local designs that is not for sale in the States.

For a few years, Western Star and DAF trucks rolled off the production line side by side in Australia. From this joint venture a cabover emerged, the Western Star Series 1000 incorporating a DAF cab and an American driveline.

International Trucks of Australia, now part of the Iveco Group, also produces models specifically for the local market. This is a recent F4670 Transtar powered by a frugal NTC 444 Cummins diesel engine.

Mack is also popular 'down-under', especially as a tractor pulling giant roadtrains. This 400HP MHR614 Ultra-Liner twinsteer truck with three trailers has a GCW of 142 tons.

A good-looking Mack RB600 is made in New Zealand, and is not to be confused with the RB construction truck in the USA. The NZ version is a unique highway model with a style of its own.

Hendrickson was taken over by HME, and as well as a range of special vehicles it still builds a highway truck too. The good-looking VT-100 Bullet is the most recent aerodynamic design.

Just like his European colleagues, the American truck driver can't complain about lack of luxury these days. The plush interior of this new Mack CH600 with integral sleeper speaks for itself.

Streamlining has also been introduced in the construction sector. The driver now has a better view of the road. This is a Kenworth T450 asphalt dumptruck in Michigan.

During the Eighties
Traksomex briefly
assembled an R-Series
Mack sporting a Super-
Liner hood in
Monterrey for the
Mexican market.

Since 1991 Freightliner
conventionals like this
FLD112SD-model have
been assembled in the
former Famsa plant in
Mexico City.

The International Paystar 5000 is still being built after 20 years. This big coal hauler has a 425HP Caterpillar diesel, Fuller RTX-14708 transmission, Rockwell axles and a 45-ton GVW.

By popular demand Marmon re-introduced a model with a long angular nose, the SB125P. The windshield has been slightly streamlined and an integral sleeper fitted to modernize it.

Freightliner has offered a 'small' truck since 1990, the Business Class. The FL80 can be had with Cummins or Mercedes-Benz diesel engines up to 275HP.

During and after the Gulf War Oshkosh received many compliments from US forces about their vehicles. The Oshkosh M1070 is a colossal new 8x8 tank transporter with a 500HP diesel unit.

Two of Peterbilt's latest aerodynamic models, the 377A/E Conventional and the 372 COE. Apart from good earning abilities these trucks offer a lot of comfort for the driver.

In 1991 Ford introduced the beautiful Aero-Max 120 in an attempt to enlarge its market share among Class 8 owner operators.

Mack's RD600 has been a bestseller in the construction industry for many years. Recently it received a redesigned front end and the option of the V-MAC electronic fuel and engine management system.

Since 1986 GMC trucks has been part of the Volvo-GM Group. It is still active in the middle and heavy truck sector, as is shown by this smart 1992 GMC TopKick tandem-axle chassis.

For the man who believes that prestige is more important than aerodynamics, Freightliner offers the FLD120 Classic. It is a custom-built truck with traditional styling offering a long list of optional extras.

In 1991 Innovisions designed the Phantom AT-X based on the Western Star 5900 model. This luxurious streamliner is powered by an electronically managed Cummins N14-460E COMMAND diesel engine.

The top model in the Mack range is the big CL600/700 longnose. This is the larger brother to the CH-Series and can be fitted with Mack, Cummins, Caterpillar or Detroit diesel engines with power ratings from 250 to 530HP.

In 1989 Peterbilt celebrated its 50th anniversary. There is a world of difference between the simple Model 334 of 1939 and the modern Model 379.

AUTHOR'S NOTE AND ACKNOWLEDGEMENTS

Many of the colour photos in this book were taken by the author himself. However, for the use of the unique pictures dating back to the Fifties and Sixties he would like to thank in particular Joe Wanchura and Neil Sherff for their great help. Both were enthusiastic truck-spotters at a very young age. Apart from black and white pictures from his own archives the author has also used much material kindly submitted by body and trailer manufacturers Fruehauf, Heil, Trailmobile, Wilson and others.

A special word of thanks should also go to Scott Anderson of Volvo-GM, Ken Elliott of Peterbilt, Peter Mosling of Oshkosh, Debra Nicholson of Freightliner and Richard Schlicting of Kenworth for their continuous support in this and other book projects of the author's. Niels Jansen is also grateful for the assistance that was given by some other truck manufacturers and/or their agencies and extends his thanks to organizations like the American Trucking Association, the American Truck Historical Society, the Goodyear Tire & Rubber Company, the Mack Museum and others.

Finally he must mention the invaluable help that was received from Michael Beesley, Steve Drybrough, Rolland Jerry, the brothers Van Ramshorst, Arie van Reeuwijk and Martin Wallast. Without the support of all these people, plus several other individuals, companies and organizations that have not been mentioned by name, this publication would not have been possible.

PHOTO INDEX

Acme 24
Autocar 7, 41, 46, 62, 78, 87, 95, 101, 108, 133
Available 27, 55, 60
Brockway 30, 36, 56, 95
Brown 54, 69, 76
CCC 102
Challenger 123
Chevrolet 30, 52, 68, 90, 96, 109
Condor 35
Corbitt 72
DAF 102, 136
Diamond T 26, 32, 33, 50, 54, 57, 62, 73, 80, 85, 96
Diamond-Reo 103
Dodge 46, 102
Dorsey 101
Fageol 11, 23, 36, 40
Federal 35, 44, 49, 50, 59, 64
Ford 14, 19, 32, 39, 68, 71, 72, 104, 122, 132, 144,
Freightliner 64, 69, 74, 86, 103, 114, 117, 120, 126, 131, 140, 143, 146
Fruehauf 13, 14, 15, 30, 44, 50, 67, 95
FWD 13, 25, 99
Gar Wood 39
GMC 13, 33, 34, 37, 39, 52, 57, 63, 74, 75, 84, 90, 93, 98, 109, 146
Goodyear 15, 19
Gramm 35
Great Dane 75
Hayes 30, 75, 93, 99, 105
Heil 14, 25, 34, 41, 47
Hendrickson 24, 77, 89, 100, 139
Henschel 63
Indiana 29
International 27, 28, 42, 46, 59, 62, 66, 76, 79, 84, 88, 91, 102, 116, 119, 137, 141
Kentucky 87
Kenworth 25, 33, 40, 47, 48, 61, 65, 65, 66, 67, 69, 76, 77, 78, 83, 98, 100, 111, 113, 124, 128, 129, 130, 133, 134, 136, 139
Knox 17
Kromhout 46
Le Moon 21

Leyland 83
Maccar 26
Mack 11, 12, 14, 16, 21, 22, 23, 25, 27, 28, 33, 36, 37, 38, 40, 49, 50, 51, 53, 54, 56, 57, 58, 61, 67, 80, 82, 86, 87, 91, 92, 94, 95, 97, 101, 104, 108, 127, 129, 138, 139, 140, 145, 148
Marmon 127, 141
Marmon-Herrington 43
Mercedes-Benz 114, 117
Oldsmobile 43
Oshkosh 16, 38, 92, 97, 100, 142
Pacific 115
Packard 5, 20
Paymaster 112
Peninsula 90
Peterbilt 40, 58, 60, 63, 70, 71, 73, 88, 107, 112, 128, 130, 132, 135, 144, 149
Pierce-Arrow 20
Reiland-Bree 27
Reo 35, 70, 77, 79, 88
Republic 22
Rubber Railway 106
Schacht 28
Scot 104
Sicard 99
Sterling 17, 21, 23, 41, 45, 47, 64, 70
Studebaker 41
Trailmobile 16, 53, 65, 94, 124
Utility 85
Volvo 118, 131
Walter 10
Ward LaFrance 55
Western Star 113, 126, 136, 148
White 10, 11, 14, 15, 18, 20, 31, 34, 35, 42, 48, 52, 60, 64, 65, 68, 69, 71, 73, 81, 94, 106, 118
White-GMC 131
Wilson 42, 86